Success in Math

General Math

Student Edition

Reviewer:
Joseph Caruso
Mathematics Department Chair
Somerville High School
Somerville, Massachusetts

Director Editorial & Marketing, Secondary Supplemental: Nancy Surridge
Market Manager: Rhonda Anderson
Executive Editor: Jean Liccione
Project Editor: Jennifer McCarthy
Editor: Laura Ring
Contributing Editors: Stephanie Petron Cahill, Elena Petron, Douglas Falk
Editorial Development: Pat Cusick and Associates
Editorial Assistant: Derrell Bradford
Production Director: Kurt Scherwatzky
Production Editors: Suzanne Keezer, John Roberts
Art Direction: Josée Ungaretta
Page Design: Margarita Giammanco
Electronic Page Production: Lesiak/Crampton Design, Inc.
Cover Design: Leslie Baker

Printed in the United States of America
 2 3 4 5 6 7 8 9 10   00 99 98

ISBN: 0-8359-1824-6

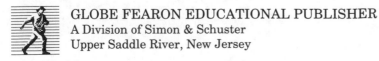
GLOBE FEARON EDUCATIONAL PUBLISHER
A Division of Simon & Schuster
Upper Saddle River, New Jersey

Contents

Chapter 1
Whole Numbers

In this chapter, you will learn

- To round whole numbers
- To estimate sums and differences
- To add and subtract whole numbers
- To estimate products and quotients
- To multiply whole numbers
- To divide whole numbers
- To use the order of operations

You or your friends may work in part-time jobs after school or during the weekends. Many jobs require that you add, subtract, multiply, or divide numbers to complete a task. For example, suppose you stock produce at the Quick Stop Grocery. Your employer has given you a list of items to stock.

Item	Amount	Shelf Space
Broccoli	3 cases	24 inches
Lettuce	28 heads	18 inches
Carrots	46 bags	14 inches
Potatoes	125 pounds	48 inches

As you stock the items, you may ask yourself questions such as these: About how many bags of carrots are there to stock? If 12 heads of lettuce are already on the shelf, how many will there be on the shelf after the new heads are stocked? If there are 26 heads of broccoli in a case, about how many heads are there to stock? Will all of the broccoli fit on the shelf if 24 heads fit in 1 foot of space? If the potatoes come in 5-pound bags, and there are already 16 bags out, how many bags will there be all together?

In this chapter you will learn the skills you need to answer questions like these that come up on the job and in everyday life.

↘ 1.1 Rounding Whole Numbers

In This Lesson, You Will Learn
To round whole numbers

Words to Learn
Approximate about how many

Rounding expressing an amount to the nearest ten, hundred, thousand, or other place value

Whole numbers the numbers 0, 1, 2, 3, 4, and so on

Place value the value of a digit according to its position in a number

Digits the 10 basic symbols used to write numbers: 0, 1, 2, 3, 4, 5, 6, 7, 8, 9

Carol works as a hostess at Mesquite Manor. She keeps a written record of the exact number of people served each night. Before she goes home, she tells her boss the **approximate** number of diners that night, or about how many people were served.

Night	People Served
Wednesday	346
Thursday	175
Friday	421
Saturday	398

New Idea

Rounding a **whole number** means expressing the number to the nearest ten, hundred, thousand, or other **place value.** When Carol reports the number of dinners served on Wednesday night, she rounds the exact number of people served.

Carol rounds 346 to 350. Because she is rounding to the nearest ten, the tens place is called the rounding place.

To round numbers without using a number line, follow these steps:

346 is closer to 350 than 340.
346 rounds to 350.

Step 1: Find the **digit** in the rounding place.

3 <u>4</u> 6

Step 2: Look at the digit to the right of the rounding place. If the digit to the right is less than 5, the digit in the rounding place stays the same. If it is 5 or more, add 1 to the digit in the rounding place.

3 4 <u>6</u>

$6 > 5$

$4 + 1 = 5$

Step 3: All the digits to the right of the digit in the rounding place become 0.

3 5 <u>0</u>

The chart below shows how Carol rounds to the tens place.

	Thursday	Friday	Saturday
Exact	1 <u>7</u> 5 (5 = 5)	4 <u>2</u> 1 (1 < 5)	3 <u>9</u> 8 (8 > 5)
Rounded	1 8 0	4 2 0	4 0 0

Follow the same steps to round to any place value.

Example: Round 1,647 to the hundreds place.

Step 1:	Find the digit in the hundreds place.	1 , <u>6</u> 4 7
Step 2:	Look at the digit to the right of it. If the digit is less than 5, the digit in the rounding place stays the same. Digits to the right of that place become 0.	1 , 6 <u>4</u> 7 4 < 5 1 , 6 0 0

Focus on the Idea

To round whole numbers, find the digit in the rounding place and look at the digit to its right. If the digit is 5 or more, add 1 to the digit in the rounding place. If the digit is less than 5, leave the digit in the rounding place alone. All digits that follow the rounding place become 0.

Practice *Show your work on a separate sheet of paper.*

Round to the tens place.

1. 66	2. 128	3. 537	4. 1,559
5. 1,071	6. 1,361	7. 4,005	8. 6,287

Round to the hundreds place.

9. 292	10. 637	11. 5,971	12. 7,339
13. 3,214	14. 1,547	15. 70,207	16. 6,295

Round to the thousands place.

17. 2,942	18. 3,010	19. 1,895	20. 2,993
21. 3,298	22. 11,679	23. 18,465	24. 21,050

Apply the Idea

The following totals were listed for each week in August. Round each week's total to the hundreds place.

25. August 5	1,741 people	26. August 12	895 people
27. August 19	2,404 people	28. August 26	1,277 people

Write About It

29. "Seventeen babies were born last night in Westmoreland. The population of Westmoreland is 38,000." In the preceding sentence, which number do you think is rounded and which number do you think is exact? Why?

1.2 Estimating Sums and Differences

In This Lesson, You Will Learn
To estimate sums and differences

Words To Learn
Estimate to find an approximate answer

Sum the answer you get when you add two or more numbers

Difference the answer you get when you subtract two numbers

Mental math doing arithmetic in your head

Kim works in CD sales at Melodyland Music. Each week she reports the 5 top-selling titles to the local radio station. Then she estimates the total sales for all 5 titles to give to her manager. How does she arrive at her estimate?

New Idea

When you **estimate**, you find an approximate answer that tells about how much or how many. One way to estimate a sum or difference is to round the numbers first and then add or subtract them. The **sum** is the number you get when you add two or more numbers and the **difference** is the number you get when you subtract them. Follow these steps to estimate the total sales or sum of each title's sales for the week.

Step 1: Round the exact amounts to the nearest hundred.

Group	Exact Sales		Rounded Sales
1. Glory Road	2,484	→	2,500
2. Highway Heart	1,741	→	1,700
3. Velvet Machine	1,277	→	1,300
4. Three Coins	895	→	900
5. Virtual Reality	734	→	700

Step 2: Use mental math to add the rounded numbers in your head.

$1,300 + 700 = 2,000$

Look for two numbers that add up to an even thousand.

Look for or make other combinations of numbers that combine easily. For instance, look at 1,700 and 900.

$$1,700 + 300 = 2,000$$
$$900 - 300 = 600$$

You can take 300 from 900 and add it to 1,700 to make 2,000.

Step 3: Use mental math to add the rounded amounts.

$$2,000 + 2,000 + 600 + 2,500 = 7,100$$

The estimate of total sales for all five titles is 7,100.

You can also estimate differences. Suppose Kim wants to estimate the difference in total dollar sales for two weeks.

Step 1: Round each number to the nearest hundred.

Step 2: Subtract to find the difference.

Week 1 $18,963 → $19,000
Week 2 $16,420 → $16,400
$19,000 − $16,400 = $2,600

Focus on the Idea

To estimate a sum or difference, round the numbers. Use mental math to add or subtract.

Practice *Show your work on a separate sheet of paper.*

Round to the nearest ten. Then estimate the sum or difference.

1.	226	2.	115	3.	44	4.	398
	+ 74		− 59		+ 63		+ 416

Round to the nearest hundred. Then estimate the sum or difference.

5.	179	6.	3,054	7.	2,710	8.	9,302
	+ 121		− 1,784		+ 1,294		− 6,799

Round to the nearest thousand. Then choose the answer that is the best estimate for the difference.

9. 12,431 − 8,974 = **a.** 2,000 **b.** 3,000 **c.** 4,400

10. 6,526 − 2,289 = **a.** 2,000 **b.** 5,000 **c.** 4,000

Apply the Idea

11. Anita needs to order hot dogs for September, based on her weekly hot dog sales in August. Estimate how many hot dogs she sold in August.

August Hot Dog Sales	
Week	Number Sold
Aug 3	551
Aug 10	324
Aug 17	434
Aug 24	696

Write About It

12. In Problem 11, do you think Anita should order the number of hot dogs she estimates, or should she order more? How might rounding affect her estimate? Explain your answer.

1.3 Adding and Subtracting Whole Numbers

In This Lesson, You Will Learn
To add and subtract whole numbers

Words to Learn
Regroup to exchange any equivalent amount for another; for example, to exchange a ten for 10 ones or a hundred for 10 tens

Hector works part-time at the video store. He keeps a chart of the number of videos checked out each day. His manager asked him to find the total number of videos checked out Monday and Tuesday.

Videos Checked Out for Week of May 15

Mon.	Tues.	Wed.	Thurs.	Fri.	Sat.	Sun.
1,335	979	909	983	1,378	2,275	1,721

New Idea
Hector can add to find the total number of videos checked out Monday and Tuesday. It is helpful to estimate first to help you tell whether your answer is accurate.

Regrouping Chart
10 ones = 1 ten
10 tens = 1 hundred
10 hundreds = 1 thousand
10 thousands = 1 ten thousand

$$1{,}335 + 979 \rightarrow 1{,}300 + 1{,}000 = 2{,}300$$

To add, line up the ones digits and regroup as necessary as you add the numbers in each column from right to left. When you **regroup**, you exchange 10 units for 1 equivalent unit as shown in the chart. Follow these steps:

Step 1:
Add ones.
Regroup.

$$\begin{array}{r} 1 \\ 1{,}335 \\ +\ 979 \\ \hline 4 \end{array}$$

Step 2:
Add tens.
Regroup.

$$\begin{array}{r} 1\ 1 \\ 1{,}335 \\ +\ 979 \\ \hline 14 \end{array}$$

Step 3:
Add hundreds.
Regroup.

$$\begin{array}{r} 1\ 1\ 1 \\ 1{,}335 \\ +\ 979 \\ \hline 314 \end{array}$$

Step 4:
Add thousands.

$$\begin{array}{r} 1\ 1\ 1 \\ 1{,}335 \\ +\ 979 \\ \hline 2{,}314 \end{array}$$

2,314 is close to the estimate of 2,300.

To find the difference between the numbers of videos checked out on Friday and Saturday, Hector subtracts. He lines up the ones digits, then he subtracts and regroups as necessary, using these steps:

Step 1:
Regroup tens.
Subtract ones.

$$\begin{array}{r} \overset{6\;15}{2,2\,7\,5} \\ -\;1,3\,7\,8 \\ \hline 7 \end{array}$$

Step 2:
Regroup hundreds.
Subtract tens.

$$\begin{array}{r} \overset{1\;16\;15}{2,2\,7\,5} \\ -\;1,3\,7\,8 \\ \hline 9\;7 \end{array}$$

Step 3:
Regroup thousands.
Subtract hundreds.

$$\begin{array}{r} \overset{1\;11\;16\;15}{2,2\,7\,5} \\ -\;1,3\,7\,8 \\ \hline 8\;9\;7 \end{array}$$

Step 4:
Subtract thousands.

$$\begin{array}{r} \overset{1\;11\;16\;15}{2,2\,7\,5} \\ -\;1,3\,7\,8 \\ \hline 8\;9\;7 \end{array}$$

Focus on the Idea

To add or subtract whole numbers, begin with the digits in the ones place. Regroup as necessary as you work from right to left.

Practice *Show your work on a separate sheet of paper.*

Add or subtract.

1. $\begin{array}{r} 45 \\ -\,18 \end{array}$
2. $\begin{array}{r} 73 \\ +\,65 \end{array}$
3. $\begin{array}{r} 179 \\ +\,21 \end{array}$
4. $\begin{array}{r} 501 \\ -\,476 \end{array}$
5. $\begin{array}{r} 600 \\ -\,399 \end{array}$

6. $\begin{array}{r} 293 \\ +\,116 \end{array}$
7. $\begin{array}{r} 4,197 \\ -\,318 \end{array}$
8. $\begin{array}{r} 2,353 \\ +\,1,647 \end{array}$
9. $\begin{array}{r} 3,000 \\ -\,2,285 \end{array}$
10. $\begin{array}{r} 12,496 \\ +\,6,782 \end{array}$

Apply the Idea

The chart below shows how many cards the library gives out in 3 months. Use it to answer Problems 11–14.

LIBRARY CARDS ISSUED

Week	June	July	August
Week 1	135	103	246
Week 2	207	141	95
Week 3	85	247	190
Week 4	158	159	201

11. How many cards did the library give out each month?
    a. June   **b.** July   **c.** August
12. How many cards were given out in total?
13. How many more cards were given out in July than in June?
14. How many more cards were given out in August than in July?

Write About It

15. Why should people learn to add and subtract when they have calculators? Explain your answer.

1.4 Estimating Products and Quotients

In This Lesson, You Will Learn

To estimate products and quotients

Words to Learn

Product the answer you get when you multiply two or more numbers

Quotient the answer you get when you divide

Armando works at Best Bakery. He sets up fresh cookies on trays every morning. A restaurant called in an order for 30 trays of cookies. If each tray holds 48 cookies, about how many cookies will Armando need to fill the order for 30 trays?

New Idea

Armando needs to estimate the **product** of 48 × 30 to find about how many cookies he will need. One way to help you estimate a product is to use rounding. To estimate the product of 48 and 30, follow these steps:

Step 1: Round to the nearest ten. $48 \rightarrow 50$

Step 2: Multiply the rounded numbers. $50 \times 30 =$

Use mental math:

First, count all the zeros. Write the same number of zeros after the = sign.

$$\underline{50} \times 3\underline{0} = \underline{00}$$

Next, multiply only the whole numbers. Write that number in front of the zero(s).

$$\underline{50} \times \underline{30} = \underline{1500} \leftarrow \text{product}$$

The product of 48 × 30 is around 1,500, so Armando needs approximately 1,500 cookies to fill 30 trays.

A local deli ordered 500 cookies from Best Bakery. The deli wants the cookies wrapped up into packages of 6. To estimate how many packages he will be making, Armando needs to find out about how many groups of 6 are in 500. To do this, he must estimate the **quotient** of 500 ÷ 6. One way to estimate a quotient is to look for numbers you know divide evenly.

Step 1: Round the numbers so they are easy to use mentally. Because 6 does not divide evenly into 50 but does divide evenly into 48, change 500 to 480.

$$500 \rightarrow 480$$

Step 2: Use mental math to divide 480 by 6.

$$480 \div 6 = 80 \leftarrow \text{quotient}$$

The quotient of $500 \div 6$ is around 80, so Armando will be making approximately 80 packages of cookies.

Focus on the Idea

To estimate a product or quotient, round one or both of the numbers. Use mental math to multiply or divide.

Practice *Show your work on a separate sheet of paper.*

Use rounding to estimate the products and quotients.

1. $\begin{array}{r} 43 \\ \times\ 6 \\ \hline \end{array}$	**2.** $\begin{array}{r} 35 \\ \times\ 11 \\ \hline \end{array}$	**3.** $\begin{array}{r} 59 \\ \times\ 48 \\ \hline \end{array}$	**4.** $\begin{array}{r} 234 \\ \times\ 150 \\ \hline \end{array}$

5. $59 \div 3$ **6.** $85 \div 13$ **7.** $410 \div 23$ **8.** $348 \div 7$

From the three choices, choose the best method to estimate the product or quotient.

9. 451×78 **a.** 450×70 **b.** 400×78 **c.** 450×80

10. $4,535 \div 83$ **a.** $5,000 \div 80$ **b.** $4,500 \div 90$ **c.** $4,500 \div 80$

Apply the Idea

11. Jay is setting up 29 tables for a reception. Each table seats 6. Estimate the number of guests expected at the reception.

12. There are 235 people attending an awards banquet. The banquet takes place in a room that holds 35 tables. Would it be better to use tables seating 8 or 6? Explain how you estimated your answer.

13. Bernie works as a dish washer after school. He earned $2,306 in 48 weeks. About how much is his weekly pay?

Write About It

14. A customer orders 17 dozen blueberry muffins from Armando's bakery. The recipe makes 160 muffins. Estimate to see whether all the muffins can be made from one recipe. Explain your answer.

◄ 1.5 Multiplying Whole Numbers

In This Lesson, You Will Learn

To multiply whole numbers

Words to Learn

Factor a number multiplied by another number to find a product

Partial product the number you get when you multiply a number by one digit of another number

---

Beth works 4 afternoons a week for a software company. She can fit 24 boxes into each carton. If she filled 3 cartons, how many boxes of software did she pack?

New Idea

If 24 boxes fit into each carton and Beth packed 3 cartons, you can find the answer by adding 24 three times.

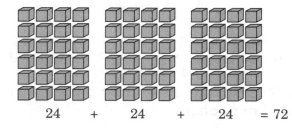

$$24 \quad + \quad 24 \quad + \quad 24 \quad = 72$$

To make the addition easier, add 3 groups of 20 and then add 3 groups of 4.

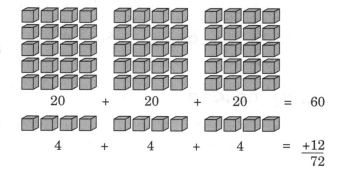

$$20 \quad + \quad 20 \quad + \quad 20 \quad = \quad 60$$

$$4 \quad + \quad 4 \quad + \quad 4 \quad = \quad \frac{+12}{72}$$

Adding many numbers takes time. To add the same number 3 times, you can multiply by 3 to find the same result.

$$3 \times 24 = 72$$
$$\uparrow \quad \uparrow$$
factors

Multiply the ones.
Regroup the ones.

$$\begin{array}{r} 1 \\ 24 \\ \times\ 3 \\ \hline 2 \end{array}$$ $4 \times 3 = 12$

Multiply the tens.
Add 1 ten.

$$\begin{array}{r} 1 \\ 24 \\ \times\ 3 \\ \hline 72 \end{array}$$ 2 tens $\times$ 3 = 6 tens
6 tens + 1 ten = 7 tens

To multiply two-digit numbers, multiply each place. Regroup and add as necessary.

Example: Multiply 24×35.

Step 1: Multiply by the ones digit. Remember to regroup. The number you get is called a **partial product.**

$$\begin{array}{r} {\scriptstyle 2} \\ 24 \\ \times\ 35 \\ \hline 120 \end{array} \leftarrow 5 \times 24$$

↑ partial product

Step 2: Multiply by the tens digit. Remember to regroup.

Step 3: Add the partial products to get the product.

The product of 24 × 35 is 840.

$$\begin{array}{r} {\scriptstyle 1} \\ {\scriptstyle \not{2}} \\ 24 \\ \times\ 35 \\ \hline 120 \\ 720 \end{array} \leftarrow 30 \times 24$$

↑ partial product

$$\begin{array}{r} {\scriptstyle 1} \\ {\scriptstyle \not{2}} \\ 24 \\ \times\ 35 \\ \hline 120 \\ +720 \\ \hline 840 \end{array}$$

Focus on the Idea

Instead of adding the same number several times, multiply. Start by multiplying by the digit in the ones place, then the tens place, and so on. Regroup numbers and add partial products where necessary.

Practice *Show your work on a separate sheet of paper.*
Multiply.

1.	2.	3.	4.	5.	6.	7.
27	63	29	94	162	334	143
× 5	× 8	× 18	× 31	× 13	× 22	×516

Complete the chart. Find the total number of boxes Beth packed each day.

	Day	Cartons	Boxes per Carton	Total Boxes Packed
8.	Tuesday	12	24	?
9.	Thursday	18	24	?
10.	Friday	24	24	?
11.	Saturday	36	24	?

Apply the Idea

12. According to the chart above, Beth packed 90 cartons. The Accounting Department budgets $500 per week to ship the cartons. If each carton costs $4 to ship, has the department budgeted enough money? Show your work and explain your answer.

Write About It

13. Step 2 of the example shows the partial product of multiplying by the tens digit as 24 × 30 = 720. Explain why the number 30 is used instead of 3 to represent the value of the tens digit.

1.6 Dividing Whole Numbers

In This Lesson, You Will Learn
To divide whole numbers

Words to Learn
Dividend the number to be divided
Divisor the number used to divide
Remainder the number left over after dividing

Greg's manager asks him to pack 432 shirts into boxes. Each box holds 16 shirts. How many boxes does he need?

New Idea
Greg needs to know how many groups of 16 there are in 432. He needs to divide the **dividend**, 432, by the **divisor**, 16. He can write the problem two different ways:

$432 \div 16$ *or*   divisor $\rightarrow 16\overline{)432}$ $\leftarrow$ dividend

Once you have set up the problem, follow these steps to divide:

Step 1: Decide where to put the first quotient digit.
16 is greater than 4.
16 is less than 43.
The first digit goes over the 3.

$$\overset{\downarrow}{}\\ 16\overline{)432}$$

Step 2: Divide 43 by 16. Estimate: $40 \div 20$.
Write 2 over the 3 in the dividend.

Step 3: Multiply 2×16. Write 32 under 43.

$$\begin{array}{r} 2 \\ 16\overline{)432} \\ -32 \\ \hline 11 \end{array}$$

Step 4: Subtract. The difference, 11, is less than 16, the divisor. The first quotient digit (2) is correct.

Step 5: Bring down the next number, 2, from the dividend.

$$\begin{array}{r} 2 \\ 16\overline{)432} \\ -32\downarrow \\ \hline 112 \end{array}$$

Step 6: Divide 112 by 16.
Estimate: $100 \div 20 = 5$.
Check estimate: $5 \times 16 = 80$.
80 is much too small. Try 7.
Multiply and subtract. The second quotient digit (7) is correct.

$432 \div 16 = 27$. Greg will need 27 boxes.

$$\begin{array}{r} 25 \\ 16\overline{)432} \\ -32\downarrow \\ \hline 112 \\ -80 \\ \hline 32 \end{array} \qquad \begin{array}{r} 27 \\ 16\overline{)432} \\ -32\downarrow \\ \hline 112 \\ -112 \\ \hline 0 \end{array}$$

Sometimes a division problem has an amount left over after you divide. The leftover number is called the **remainder.**

Example: Greg needs to pack 540 sweaters into boxes. Each box holds 24 sweaters. Find the number of boxes he needs.

Step 1: Decide where to put the first quotient digit. 24 is less than 54, so the first digit goes over the 4.

Step 2: Divide 54 by 24. Estimate: 50 ÷ 20 is about 2. Write 2 over the 4 in the dividend.

$$
\begin{array}{r}
2 \\
24\overline{)540} \\
-48{\downarrow} \\
\hline
60
\end{array}
$$

Step 3: Multiply 2 × 24. Write 48 under 54. Subtract and bring down the next number from the dividend.

Step 4: Divide 60 by 24. Write 2 over 0 in the dividend. Multiply 2 × 24. Write 48 under 60.

Step 5: Subtract. You have a remainder of 12. Write the remainder in the dividend after R.

$$
\begin{array}{r}
22\ \text{R12} \\
24\overline{)540} \\
-48{\downarrow} \\
\hline
60 \\
-48 \\
\hline
12
\end{array}
$$

540 ÷ 24 = 22 R12, so Greg will need 23 boxes to hold all the sweaters: 22 will be full and the 23rd will have the remaining 12 sweaters.

Focus on the Idea

The basic sequence of steps in a division problem is as follows: divide, multiply, subtract, and bring down.

Practice *Show your work on a separate sheet of paper.*

Divide.

1. 64 ÷ 2
2. 98 ÷ 5
3. 126 ÷ 9
4. 504 ÷ 8

5. 225 ÷ 15
6. 729 ÷ 28
7. 1,236 ÷ 3
8. 3,000 ÷ 10

9. 4)27
10. 3)405
11. 19)437
12. 16)2,840

Apply the Idea

13. If Greg has 162 boxes and he can fit 12 boxes on a shelf, how many shelves will he need to hold all the boxes?

Write About It

14. Suppose you put a guitar that costs $498 on layaway. You must pay it off in 6 months. How can dividing help you decide how much to pay each month? Explain your answer and show your work.

In This Lesson, You Will Learn

To use the order of operations

Words to Learn

Operation addition, subtraction, multiplication, or division

Order of operations the rules that determine the order in which you add, subtract, multiply, or divide

Parentheses ( ) symbols used to group numbers and operations

Erin works in the mail-order department of a music company. She was asked to fill the order on the right. Erin finds all of the material in stock, so she totals the order to prepare it for shipping. There is also a $4 handling charge for each order. Erin writes:

Order to Fill	
Quantity	**Merchandise**
3	cassette tapes @ $6 each
5	CDs @ $12 each

Total = $3 \times 6 + 5 \times 12 + 4$

Erin calculates $280 for the cost of the order. $280 is high for such a small order. She goes back to the original order to find her mistake. How did she end up with such a big number?

New Idea

There is a special order that must be followed when solving problems with more than one **operation**. Multiplication and division must be done before addition and subtraction. The order is called the **order of operations**.

Erin should have multiplied before she added.

Step 1: Multiply first.

Step 2: Add.

$3 \times 6 + 5 \times 12 + 4 = 82$, so the total price is $82.

Qty.	Item	Price
1	2637-Tape	$6.00
1	4222-Tape	$6.00
1	1987-Tape	$6.00
1	4663-CD	$12.00
1	1244-CD	$12.00
1	0987-CD	$12.00
1	7742-CD	$12.00
1	5526-CD	$12.00
8	Order Totals	$78.00
	Handling fee	$4.00
	Total due	$82.00

$$\underbrace{3 \times 6}_{18} + \underbrace{5 \times 12}_{60} + 4$$
$$\underbrace{18 + 60}_{78} + 4$$
$$78 + 4 = 82$$

When a problem has only addition and subtraction, work from left to right.

Example: Find the value of $16 - 9 + 3$.

Subtract $\underbrace{16 - 9}_{} + 3$

Add. $\underbrace{7 \quad + 3}_{}$

                 10

$16 - 9 + 3 = 10$

Always multiply and divide from left to right before adding or subtracting.

Example: Find the value of $36 - 16 \div 2 \times 4 + 5$.

Step 1: Multiply and divide from left to right.
Divide first. $36 - \underbrace{16 \div 2}_{} \times 4 + 5$

Step 2: Multiply. $36 - \underbrace{8 \quad \times 4}_{} + 5$

Step 3: Add and subtract from left to right.
Subtract first. $\underbrace{36 - \qquad\quad 32}_{} \quad + 5$

Step 4: Add. $4 \qquad\qquad + 5 = 9$

$36 - 16 \div 2 \times 4 + 5 = 9$

 Some calculators follow the order of operations and some do not. To find out whether your calculator follows the order of operations, enter the following problem just as it is written.

36   ⊟   16   ⊡   2   ⊠   4   ⊞   5   ⊜

If your calculator shows 9 as the answer, it is a *scientific calculator* and follows the order of operations.

If your calculator shows 45, it does not follow the order of operations. When you use this kind of calculator, you must decide which operations to do first. Write each answer down so that you can rekey it into the calculator to perform the next operation, just as you did in the example.

✓ Check the Math

A student calculated the following problem. What did the student do wrong? Correct the mistake.

     $\underbrace{12 + 3}_{} - \underbrace{6 + 2}_{}$

       $\underbrace{15 \quad - \quad 8}_{}$

          7

Focus on the Idea

There is an order of operations that must be followed when solving problems.
    First, multiply and divide from left to right.
    Then, add and subtract from left to right.

Practice *Show your work on a separate sheet of paper.*

Find the value using the order of operations.

1. $14 + 18 \times 2$ 2. $9 - 15 \div 5$ 3. $27 + 6 - 2$

4. $36 \div 3 \times 6$ 5. $23 - 6 + 5$ 6. $20 + 3 - 16 + 5$

7. $12 + 8 \times 6 - 6 \times 2$ 8. $12 \times 6 - 3 \times 7$ 9. $38 + 6 \times 9 \div 2 - 3$

Extend the Idea

Parentheses can change the order of operations. Always do the work inside the parentheses first. Then follow the order of operations.

Example 1: $4 \times (8 + 2)$
$4 \times \quad 10$
40

Example 3: $(8 + 3) \times (12 \div 3)$
$11 \quad \times \quad 4$
44

Example 2: $5 \times (8 \div 2)$
$5 \times \quad 4$
20

Example 4: $(12 - 3 \times 3) + 6$
$12 - \quad 9 \quad + 6$
$3 \quad\quad + 6$
9

You can see that parentheses in an arithmetic problem say, "Do this part first!" When you see parentheses in an expression, always do the operations within them first.

✓ Check Your Understanding

Look at the math sentence below. Rewrite and insert one set of parentheses to make the sentence true.

$10 + 4 \times 3 = 42$

 If you do not have a scientific calculator and you want to use your calculator to find the value of a problem, you will have to follow the order of operations yourself and rewrite the problem as you go.

Example: Find the value of $15 \times (47 + 85)$.

Step 1: Do the work inside the parentheses first.   47 ⊞ 85 🟰 132

Step 2: Rewrite the problem. 15×132

Step 3: Multiply.   15 ☒ 132 🟰 1,980

$15 \times (47 + 85) = 1,980$

Practice *Show your work on a separate sheet of paper.*

Find the value using order of operations.

10. $3 \times (8 + 2)$ **11.** $18 - (5 + 6)$ **12.** $13 \times (16 \div 4)$

13. $4 + (3 - 1) \times 6$ **14.** $54 \div 6 + (7 - 2)$ **15.** $32 \div (4 \times 8) + 7$

16. $25 - 3 \times (2 + 5)$ **17.** $3 \times (6 + 4) \div 5 - 6$ **18.** $(35 - 21) + 6 \div (2 \times 3)$

 Find the value using the order of operations.

19. $23 \times (146 - 89)$ **20.** $119 + 45 \times 3$ **21.** $198 \div 33 \times 28$

22. $209 + 160 + 16 \times 3$ **23.** $(116 - 31) \div (60 \div 12)$ **24.** $18 \times (45 \div 5)$

25. $88 \div (168 \div 21)$ **26.** $(56 + 49) \times (119 - 48)$ **27.** $72 \times 25 \div 12 \times 10$

Apply the Idea

28. Erin just stored 8 CDs on a shelf. She still has 5 boxes of CDs that need to be stored on the same shelf. Each box holds 18 CDs. How many CDs does she have all together?

     a. Show your work.

     b. Explain your answer.

29. A theater sold 40 tickets for \$12 and 100 tickets for \$8. How much money did the theater make in ticket sales? Show how you used the order of operations.

30. The manager in a paint store packs a box with an order for 5 cans of red paint, 3 cans of blue paint, and 1 can of white paint. Each can weighs 11 pounds. What is the total weight of the contents of the box? Write the problem using parentheses. Solve the problem.

31. Marilyn buys 3 cups of lemon yogurt and 2 cups of chocolate yogurt. Each cup costs \$2. How much do all 5 cups cost? Show how you used the order of operations.

Write About It

32. Why do we have to follow the order of operations? What would happen if we did not?

Chapter 1 Review

In this chapter, you have learned
- To round whole numbers
- To estimate sums and differences
- To add and subtract whole numbers
- To estimate products and quotients
- To multiply whole numbers
- To divide whole numbers
- To use the order of operations

Words You Know

From the lists of Words to Learn, choose the word or phrase that best completes each statement.

1. The answer you get when you divide is the ___.

2. An ___ number tells about how many.

3. The rules that determine the order in which you add, subtract, multiply, or divide are called the ___.

4. The ___ is the number used to divide.

5. A number multiplied by another number to find a product is a ___.

6. ___ is expressing an amount to the nearest ten, hundred, thousand, or other place value.

7. The answer you get when you multiply 2 or more numbers is the ___.

8. The ___ is the number to be divided.

More Practice *Show your work on a separate sheet of paper.*

Round to the nearest ten.

9. 23 10. 145 11. 1,026 12. 504 13. 298

Round to the nearest hundred.

14. 437 15. 209 16. 1,361 17. 3,975 18. 2,058

Round to the nearest thousand.

19. 1,037 20. 14,495 21. 3,600 22. 19,623

Estimate each sum or difference. Then calculate the exact answer.

23. $98 + 47$ **24.** $106 + 53$ **25.** $368 - 210$ **26.** $3,036 + 399$

27. $1,008 - 489$ **28.** $3,480 + 520$ **29.** $6,322 + 2,639$ **30.** $4,509 - 3,823$

Estimate each product or quotient. Then calculate the exact answer.

31. 14×9 **32.** 23×35 **33.** $129 \div 13$ **34.** 93×26

35. $500 \div 68$ **36.** 235×16 **37.** $2,564 \div 52$ **38.** $1,039 \times 48$

39. $2,382 \div 21$ **40.** 637×204 **41.** $23,407 \div 42$ **42.** 484×265

Find the value using the order of operations.

43. $3 + 5 \times 4$ **44.** $20 - 12 + 3$ **45.** $23 + 5 - 10 + 3$

46. $20 \div 5 \times 3$ **47.** $3 \times (7 + 3)$ **48.** $(2 + 3) \times (4 + 6)$

49. $(8 \times 3) \div (3 \times 4)$ **50.** $20 - (18 - 12)$ **51.** $28 + 16 \div 4 - 3$

52. $24 \div (6 \times 4)$ **53.** $4 + (19 - 6) \times 4$ **54.** $24 \div 4 \times 2 \div 3$

Problems You Can Solve

The following list of items to stock appeared at the beginning of this chapter. Use it to answer Problems 55–58.

Item	Amount	Shelf Space
Broccoli	3 cases	24 inches
Lettuce	28 heads	18 inches
Carrots	46 bags	14 inches
Potatoes	125 pounds	48 inches

55. What is the total shelf space for all of the vegetables?

56. If there are 26 heads of broccoli in a case, estimate how many heads there are to stock.

57. If the potatoes come in 5-pound bags, how many bags are there to stock?

58. If there are already 16 bags of potatoes on the shelf and then the new shipment is added, how many pounds of potatoes will there be on the shelf all together?

Estimate each sum or difference. Then calculate the exact answer.

1. $\begin{array}{r} 31 \\ -16 \end{array}$

2. $\begin{array}{r} 94 \\ +57 \end{array}$

3. $\begin{array}{r} 103 \\ -45 \end{array}$

4. $\begin{array}{r} 397 \\ +602 \end{array}$

5. $\begin{array}{r} 185 \\ +127 \end{array}$

6. $\begin{array}{r} 436 \\ +264 \end{array}$

7. $\begin{array}{r} 1,001 \\ -582 \end{array}$

8. $\begin{array}{r} 6,235 \\ -5,799 \end{array}$

Estimate each product or quotient. Then calculate the exact answer.

9. $\begin{array}{r} 42 \\ \times 26 \end{array}$

10. $\begin{array}{r} 185 \\ \times 131 \end{array}$

11. $6\overline{)762}$

12. $15\overline{)382}$

Find the value using the order of operations.

13. $36 \div 3 \times 4$

14. $17 - 5 \times 2$

15. $15 \times (3 + 2) - 6$

16. $12 - 3 + 10 - 3$

17. $25 - (4 + 5) \times 2$

18. $12 + 6 \times 3$

19. $18 - (10 - 2)$

20. $5 \times 6 \div (2 \times 5)$

A sports company sends a shipment of shorts to a customer. The packing list shows what the company sent. Use the list to answer Problems 21–26.

Color	Size	Quantity
Blue	Small	298
	Medium	635
	Large	416
Black	Small	572
	Large	1,589

21. Rounding to the nearest hundred, about how many blue shorts did the company send?

22. Rounding to the nearest ten, about how many more blue large shorts did the company send than small?

23. Exactly how many large shorts did the company send?

24. If the company sells the shorts for $3 each, estimate to the nearest hundred how much all the black, small shorts will cost.

25. The company sent 5 boxes of blue, medium shorts. How many shorts were in each box?

26. It cost $8 each to send 17 large boxes and $6 dollars each to send 22 medium boxes. How much did it cost in all?

Chapter 2
Decimals

In this chapter, you will learn

- To compare and order decimals
- To estimate sums and differences of decimals
- To add and subtract decimals
- To estimate products and quotients of decimals
- To multiply decimals
- To divide decimals

No matter how you travel, there are times when you need to calculate costs, distances, or the amount of fuel needed to get from one point to another. Travel-related activities, and many others, require that you work with decimals.

Kevin and 3 friends are going on a hiking trip to Clapton State Park in the White Bear Mountains. Kevin has already mapped out the trip, including a stop for lunch in the town of Clarksville, and he is making a chart that lists some of the information he already knows and some he needs to find out.

Travel Expenses	
Average mileage	27.5 miles/gallon
Tank size	14.6 gallons
Miles per tank	
Price of gas	$1.19/gallon
Distance one way	
Estimated gas expense	

About how much longer is the second leg of the trip than the first? How many miles is the trip from home to Clapton State Park? Can the trip to the park be made on 1 tank of gas? About how much money should Kevin plan to spend on gas for the entire trip? If the hikers want to complete the trail in 3 days, about how many miles should they plan to walk each day?

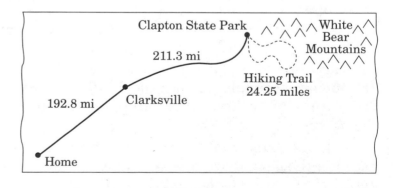

In this chapter you will learn how to find the answers to these and other travel-related questions involving money and various units of measurement that can be expressed in decimals.

2.1 Comparing and Ordering Decimals

In This Lesson, You Will Learn

To compare and order decimals

Words to Learn

Decimal a number written with a dot

Decimal point a dot used to separate a whole number from a part less than a whole. Values to the right of the dot are less than 1.

Maria requested a list of short hikes near her home. She received a list of three different trails with three different distances. She wants to try the longest one first. Which one should she take?

Wild Basin Trail	2.45 miles
Piney Woods Trail	2.09 miles
Oceanside Trail	2.7 miles

New Idea

To find the longest trail, Maria needs to compare **decimals**, the name given to any number written with a dot, or **decimal point**. The digits to the left of the decimal point are whole numbers. The digits to the right of the decimal point have values less than 1. Look at the picture of the number 2.45.

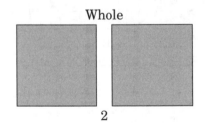

Whole   Tenths   Hundredths

2   .4   .05

2 and 4 tenths and 5 hundredths is written as 2.45 and is read as 2 and 45 hundredths.

You can also use a place value chart to find the values of decimals. To compare decimals, line up the decimal points and compare the digits from left to right until you find one digit that is larger than the others.

Look at decimals on the place value chart. The digits in the ones place are the same. 7 is the largest digit in the tenths place, so 2.7 has the greatest value. 4 is the next largest digit in the tenths place, so 2.45 has the next greatest value. 2.09 miles is the smallest number.

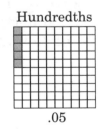

tens	ones	.	tenths	hundredths	thousandths
	2	.	4	5	
	2	.	0	9	
	2	.	7		

Placing decimals on a number line also helps you to compare numbers. Between the whole numbers are the decimals.

Example: Maria saw two different trails: One was marked 1.3 miles and the other was marked 1.30 miles. Which one is longer?

1.3 and 1.30 have the same value, so the trails are the same length.

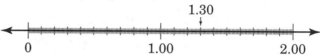

The zero in 1.30 has no value. You can add zeros as placeholders at the end of any decimal without changing the value.

 Focus on the Idea

When comparing decimals, line up the decimal points and compare digits from left to right.

Practice *Show your work on a separate sheet of paper.*
Order the numbers in each set from least to greatest.

1. 3.36, 3.64, 3.59
2. 21.97, 21.79, 22.97

3. 43, 43.22, 43.022
4. 1.03, 2.53, 0.253

5. 6.401, 0.104, 0.004
6. 5.18, 5.181, 5.081

Apply the Idea

7. Donna looked up the best times for several sprinters. List the sprinters from fastest to slowest.

Women's 200M: Final		
Athlete	**Country**	**Time**
Mary Onyali	Nigeria	22.38
Inger Miller	USA	22.41
Marie-José Pérec	France	22.12

 **Write About It**

8. How would you explain to a friend why the value of .1 is greater than .09?

2.2 Estimating Sums and Differences of Decimals

In This Lesson, You Will Learn
To estimate sums and differences of decimals

Words to Learn
Approximate number an inexact but useful number

Estimate to find an approximate answer

Rounding expressing an amount to the nearest ten, hundred, thousand, or other place value

Sum the answer you get when you add two or more numbers

Difference the answer you get when you subtract two numbers

Chau drives from Caspar to Hornfield through several towns. A map shows the distances in miles between towns.

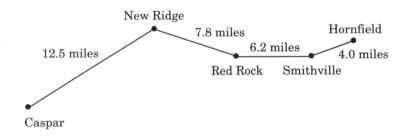

About how many miles is it from Caspar to Hornfield?

New Idea
Chau needs to know only the **approximate number** of miles, or about how far, she has to travel. An exact amount is not necessary. You can **estimate** by first **rounding** the decimals to whole numbers. Rounding decimals is almost the same as rounding whole numbers. Round 12.5 miles to the nearest whole mile.

Step 1: Look at the digit to the right of the ones place.

$12.\underline{5}$ mi

Step 2: If it is 5 or more, add 1 to the digit in the rounding place. If it is less than 5, leave the digit in rounding place alone.

$5 = 5$

Step 3: Drop the digits to the right of the rounding place.

$12.5 \rightarrow 13$ miles

12.5 rounds to 13 miles.

To estimate the total distance, or the approximate **sum** of the miles, between Caspar and Hornfield, follow these steps:

Step 1: First, round the decimals of the distances between towns to the nearest whole number.

Caspar to New Ridge	12.5 → 13
New Ridge to Red Rock	7.8 → 8
Red Rock to Smithville	6.2 → 6
Smithville to Hornfield	4.0 → 4

Step 2: Then add. Use mental math to find the sum.

It is about 31 miles from Caspar to Hornfield. $13 + 8 + 6 + 4 = 31$

You estimate a **difference** the same way you estimate a sum.

Example: Chau starts her trip with $16.50. She buys $11.67 worth of gas. Estimate how much money she has left.

Step 1: Round to the nearest whole number. $16.50 → 17$ $11.67 → 12$

Step 2: Subtract the rounded numbers to find the difference. $17 - 12 → 5$

Chau has about $5.00 left.

Focus on the Idea

Estimate the sums and differences of decimals as you would whole numbers. Round to the given place value. Then add or subtract.

Practice *Show your work on a separte sheet of paper.*
Round the decimals to whole numbers. Then estimate the sums.

1. $124.5 + 34.3$
2. $8.3 + 9.7$
3. $7.04 + 16.1$

4. $12.59 + 6.42
5. $9.80 + 1.16
6. $29.95 + 11.85

Round the decimals to whole numbers. Then estimate the differences.

7. $12.80 - 7.95$
8. $19.25 - 4.80$
9. $16.40 - 6.19$

10. $38.12 - 23.70
11. $74.43 - 9.99
12. $49.95 - 14.63

Apply the Idea
13. The map shows a different route Chau tried. Round the numbers. Estimate the total distance. Then estimate the difference between this route and the one on page 24.

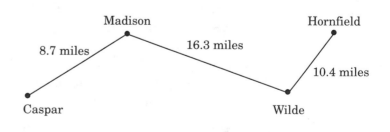

Write About It
14. When they are buying several items at a time, some people estimate the total cost before getting into the checkout line. What are the advantages of doing this? Explain.

2.3 Adding and Subtracting Decimals

In This Lesson, You Will Learn
To add and subtract decimals

Words to Learn
Budget a plan for spending money

Fernando has $400 a month to spend on his car. He makes a **budget** to plan how to spend it. To find out how much he spends each month on gas, insurance, and maintenance, Fernando uses a chart. How can he find out how much he has left over for other expenses?

May Car Expenses	
Car insurance	$209.85
Car maintenance	$37.25
Gasoline	$132.50
Other expenses	

New Idea

Fernando must first add the known expenses, and then subtract the sum from the $400 budget to find the amount of money left over. You add and subtract money, or other decimals, as you would whole numbers. Write the numbers in a column so that the decimal points line up under each other. Then add or subtract.

To complete Fernando's chart, follow these steps:

Step 1: Write all of the decimals you are adding in a column. Line up the decimal points. Add as you would add whole numbers. Remember to place a decimal point in the answer.

$$
\begin{array}{r}
^{1\,1\ \ 1} \\
\$\ 209.85 \\
\$\ 132.50 \\
+\ \$\ \ \ 37.25 \\
\hline
\$\ 379.60
\end{array}
$$

Fernando's known car expenses →

Step 2: Subtract Fernando's known expenses from his budgeted amount ($400). Because 400 is a whole number, add 2 zeros as placeholders to the right of the decimal point. Remember to write a decimal point in the answer.

$$
\begin{array}{r}
\$400.00 \\
-\ \$379.60 \\
\hline
\$\ 20.40
\end{array}
$$

← Insert placeholders

Fernando has $20.40 available for other expenses.

Focus on the Idea

Add and subtract decimals as you would whole numbers. Line up the decimal points. Use zeros as placeholders when necessary. Include a decimal point in your answer.

Practice *Show your work on a separate sheet of paper.*

Add.

1. $.45 + .33$

2. $\$.71 + \$1.55$

3. $6 + 1.4$

4. $16.83 + 5.13$

5. $.67 + 4.19$

6. $4.5 + .151$

7. $\$7.98 + \$8.03$

8. $2.983 + .714$

Subtract.

9. $3.94 - 2.17$

10. $\$9.00 - \$4.70$

11. $\$19.50 - \$7.60$

12. $34 - 2.9$

13. $\$14.70 - \$9.83$

14. $20.55 - 1.14$

15. $\$16.20 - \$3.10$

16. $.3 - .006$

Apply the Idea

Use the chart of Fernando's gasoline receipts to answer Problems 17–20. First estimate each answer. Then find the exact amount.

17. How much money did Fernando spend on May 9 and May 15 combined?

18. How much more money did Fernando spend on May 17 than on May 23?

Date	Cost
May 9	$18.94
May 15	$10.15
May 17	$19.08
May 23	$14.35

19. What is Fernando's total gasoline expense for the month of May?

20. If Fernando spends exactly the same amount for gas in June and July as he did in May, what will be the total for all 3 months?

Write About It

21. People often budget the upcoming month's gas expenses based on what they spent in the previous month. When is this a good idea? When is it not a good idea? Explain.

2.4 Estimating Products and Quotients of Decimals

In This Lesson, You Will Learn

To estimate products and quotients of decimals

Words to Learn

Product the answer you get when you multiply two or more numbers

Quotient the answer you get when you divide two numbers

Raoul is taking orders for tickets to the next football game. A total of 29 students in five homerooms have already ordered. Tickets cost $6.75 each. Raoul wants to find out approximately what ticket sales will be.

Homeroom	Tickets Ordered
101	6
102	1
103	9
104	10
105	3
Total tickets ordered	**29**

New Idea

To estimate the money from ticket sales, Raoul must multiply the approximate number of ticket buyers by the approximate cost of a ticket. To estimate the **product** of decimals, round each factor to a whole number and multiply. Follow these steps:

Step 1: Round the whole number (29) to the nearest ten. Round the decimal (6.75) to the next whole number or dollar.

$$29 \rightarrow 30$$
$$\$6.75 \rightarrow \$7$$

Step 2: Use mental math to multiply the numbers.

$$30 \times \$7 = \$210$$

Ticket sales will be approximately $210.

To estimate **quotients**, change the dividend and divisor to numbers that are easy to divide.

Example: Seven students held a fundraiser and made $129.85. If the money is divided evenly, estimate how much each student will make.

Step 1: Find a number close to 129.85 that can be divided easily by the divisor 7. 140 is the easiest whole number.

$$129.85 \rightarrow 140$$

Step 2: Divide the new dividend (140) by the divisor (7).

$$140 \div 7 = 20$$

Each student made about $20.

Because you made the divisor, or the amount to be divided, bigger than it really was, each student actually made a little less than $20.

Focus on the Idea

Estimate the products and quotients of decimals as you would whole numbers. Round to the nearest whole number, then multiply for a product or divide for a quotient.

Practice *Show your work on a separate sheet of paper.*

Raoul makes a list of expenses for the group of 29 students going to the football game. Round each expense to the nearest dollar. Use the list to estimate answers to Problems 1–3.

1. About how much money will the group need for everyone to eat lunch?

2. If the group decides to hire a bus, about how much money will each student have to pay?

3. If the group decides to use cars, about how much would each student pay?

Expense	Cost
Lunch (per person)	$4.85
Hire a bus	$150.21
Gas and parking (6 cars)	$119.90

Apply the Idea

The 29 students held a bake sale to earn money for transportation to the game. Below is a list of items for sale and their cost. Round the cost of each item. Then answer Problems 4–7.

4. The students hope to make at least $60 selling cakes. About how many cakes do they need to sell to meet their goal?

5. The students hope to make another $45 in pie sales. Estimate how many pies they need to sell to do it.

6. The bake sale makes $176.55. Estimate how much money each of the 29 students will get toward the cost of transportation.

Prices	
Drinks	$.85
Whole cake	$9.75
Whole pie	$14.99

Write About It

7. The students have 48 drinks to sell. When they round to the nearest dollar, they estimate they will make $48 if they sell all the drinks. Will they actually make more or less than $48 if they sell all the drinks? Explain.

2.5 Multiplying Decimals

In This Lesson, You Will Learn
To multiply decimals

Words to Learn
Rate the cost per unit

Rate of exchange the rate for trading money from one country for money from another country

---

Juan and Mike are going to Mexico City with their class. They have $680 to spend. Because all prices in Mexico are given in Mexican pesos, they need to find out how much $680 is worth in pesos. To help them calculate, their teacher told them to use this rule:

Dollars × Rate of Exchange = Pesos

They know the **rate of exchange** is $1 = 7.53 pesos. How can they calculate the number of pesos?

New Idea

To convert dollars to pesos, Juan and Mike have to multiply by a decimal exchange rate (7.53). To multiply decimals, first multiply the way you would with whole numbers. After finding the product, count the total number of decimal places in all the factors. In the product, count over that same number of places from the right, and write the decimal point.

To find out how many pesos $680 is worth if the exchange rate is $1 = 7.53 pesos, follow these steps:

Step 1: Multiply as with whole numbers.

Step 2: After calculating the product, count the decimal places in the factors you multiplied. Place a decimal point in the product by starting at the right and counting over the total number of places.

$680 is worth 5,120.40 pesos.

$$
\begin{array}{r}
\text{U.S. dollars} \quad \$6\,8\,0 \\
\text{Rate of exchange} \quad \times\,7.5\,3 \quad \text{2 places} \\
\hline
2\,0\,4\,0 \\
3\,4\,0\,0\,0 \\
4\,7\,6\,0\,0\,0 \\
\hline
\text{Product} \quad 5\,1\,2\,0.4\,0 \quad \text{2 places}
\end{array}
$$

Calculators have a special decimal key ⟨.⟩ to use when entering decimal numbers. Be sure to press the decimal key at the exact place it appears in the decimal number. To find the number of pesos in $680 using an exchange rate of 7.53:

680 ⟨×⟩ 7 ⟨.⟩ 53 ⟨=⟩ 5,120.4

Focus on the Idea

Multiply decimals as you would whole numbers and find the product. Then count the total number of decimal places in both factors. Count over that same number of places in the product, starting from the right. Write the decimal point.

Practice *Show your work on a separate sheet of paper.*

Multiply.

1. 27 × .04
2. 1.62 × .3
3. 10 × .06
4. 100 × 1.35

5. 3.01 × 2.7
6. 42.3 × .5
7. .1 × .3
8. 21 × .33

9. .25 × 100
10. 38 × 1.5
11. 15 × .01
12. .2 × .2

Multiply the dollar amount by the rate of exchange given.

13. $450.50   Rate: 1.23 Swiss Franc

14. $322.60   Rate: .64 British Pound

15. $235.00   Rate: 1.70 Netherland Guilder

16. $435.75   Rate: 109.00 Japanese Yen

 Multiply.

17. 158.75 × 2.50
18. 24.64 × 17.20

19. 78.45 × .67
20. 568.75 × .58

Apply the Idea

21. The Hiking Club is planning a trip to Turnback Canyon, about 110 miles away. They drive for 1.5 hours at a rate of 55 miles per hour before stopping.

    a. How many miles have they driven so far?

    b. How many more miles will they drive before arriving at the park?

Write About It

22. Find the cost of buying 6.3 gallons of gasoline at $1.09 per gallon. Explain why you need to round the product to find how much you pay.

2.6 Dividing Decimals

In This Lesson, You Will Learn
To divide decimals

Words to Learn
Divisor the number used to divide
Dividend the number to be divided

Carl's car has a gas tank that holds 17.25 gallons of gasoline. Carl drove 441.6 miles on 1 tank of gas. He wants to find the number of miles per gallon he gets when driving on the highway, so he needs to divide the total number of miles by the number of gallons in the tank.

New Idea
Carl has to divide using decimals.

$$\textbf{divisor} \rightarrow 17.25\overline{)441.6} \leftarrow \textbf{dividend}$$

In any division problem, if you multiply the dividend and divisor by the same number, the quotient stays the same.

$$6 \div 3 = 2 \quad \text{and} \quad 60 \div 30 = 2 \quad \text{and} \quad 600 \div 300 = 2$$

You can use this idea to divide with decimals. First make the divisor a whole number by multiplying by 10, 100, or 1,000. Count the number of decimal places to help you decide which number to multiply by to make the decimal into a whole number. Multiplying by 10 is the same as moving the decimal point to the right 1 place, multiplying by 100 is the same as moving it 2 places, and so on.

17.25 has 2 decimal places, so multiply by 100 → 17.25 × 100 = 1,725

If you multiply the divisor by 100, you must also multiply the dividend by 100.

441.6 × 100 = 44,160

Look at how you solve this problem from start to finish.

Step 1: Move the decimal point in the divisor to the right to make it a whole number. Move the decimal point in the dividend to the right the same number of places.

$$1725.\overline{)44160.}$$

Step 2: Write a decimal point in the quotient above the one in the dividend.

$$1,725\overline{)44,160}.$$

Step 3: Divide as you would whole numbers. Add zeros in the dividend as you need them.

Carl gets 25.6 miles per gallon on the highway.

$$
\begin{array}{r}
25.6 \\
1725\overline{)44{,}160.0} \\
-34\,50 \\
\hline
966\,0 \\
-862\,5 \\
\hline
103\,50 \\
103\,50 \\
\hline
0
\end{array}
$$

 When you divide by decimals with a calculator, you do not have to change the divisor to a whole number. For example, divide 17.5 by .13:

17 ⬚.⬚ 5 ⬚÷⬚ ⬚.⬚ 13 ⬚=⬚ 134.61538

You often get many decimal places. Unless you are told otherwise, you can round to the nearest hundredth.

17.5 ÷ .13 = 134.62

Focus on the Idea

To divide by decimals, move the decimal point in the divisor to the right as many places as needed to make it a whole number. Move the decimal point in the dividend the same number of places to the right. Divide as you would whole numbers.

Practice *Show your work on a separate sheet of paper.*
Divide.

1. $0.7\overline{)21.77}$
2. $0.63\overline{)0.0252}$
3. $1.22\overline{)4.392}$
4. $14.40 \div 4.5$
5. $5.4 \div 0.12$
6. $6.21 \div 100$

Apply the Idea

7. Edward has $17 to buy gasoline. The prices per gallon of three grades of gas are listed below. For each grade, find the number of gallons Edward could buy with his $17. Round each number of gallons to the hundredths place.

   a. Unleaded gasoline: $1.12/gallon
   b. Super unleaded gasoline: $1.23/gallon
   c. Premium gasoline: $1.36/gallon

8. Edward's car holds 15.04 gallons of gas. Can Edward fill his tank completely with $17 worth of super-unleaded gasoline? Show how you found the answer.

Write About It

9. In what other types of real-life situations might you need to divide decimals? Give at least one example and write a sample division problem to go with it.

In this chapter, you have learned

- To compare and order decimals
- To estimate sums and differences of decimals
- To add and subtract decimals
- To estimate products and quotients of decimals
- To multiply decimals
- To divide decimals

Words You Know

From the lists of Words to Learn, choose the word or phrase that best completes each statement.

1. The ___ is the answer you get adding two or more numbers.

2. You find an approximate answer when you ___.

3. A ___ is a dot used to separate a whole number from a part less than a whole.

4. A plan for spending money is called a ___ .

5. The ___ is the number to be divided.

6. The answer you get when you multiply two or more numbers is the ___.

More Practice *Show your work on a separate sheet of paper.*

Order the numbers in each set from least to greatest.

7. 5, .05, .5
8. 1.30, 1.09, 1.5
9. .05, .009, .065
10. .31, .02, .15

Match the decimal with the corresponding letter on the number line.

11. 1.5
12. .78
13. 1.99
14. 1.30
15. 1.45

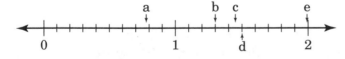

Find the sum or difference.

16. $1.34 + 3.25$
17. $11.8 - 6.2$
18. $45.21 + 2.39$
19. $\$1.50 - \$.75$

20. $1.98 + 6.02$
21. $\$4.00 - \$.75$
22. $.109 + .92$
23. $1.05 - .321$

24. $12.4 + 7.6$
25. $3.99 + .01$
26. $.103 - .009$
27. $1 - .02$

Find the product or quotient.

28. $35.2 \times .02$ **29.** $15.6 \div 1.3$ **30.** 2.5×2.5 **31.** $114.38 \div 1.9$

32. $.25 \times .8$ **33.** $67.9 \div 1.94$ **34.** $.23 \times 100$ **35.** 5.9×100

36. $11.09 \times .3$ **37.** $118.2 \div .04$ **38.** $.9 \div 10$ **39.** $6.5 \times .5$

 Problems You Can Solve

At the beginning of this chapter, you looked at some examples of ways Kevin needed to use decimal numbers to plan his hiking trip to Clapton State Park. Use the partially completed travel expenses chart and the map below to help you answer Problems 40–47.

Travel Expenses	
Average mileage	27.5 miles/gallon
Tank size	14.6 gallons
Miles per tank	
Price of gas	$1.19/gallon
Distance one way	
Estimated gas expense	

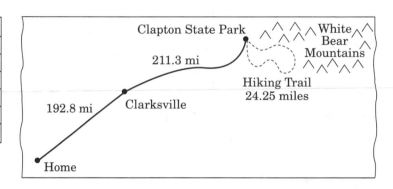

40. Which part of the trip covers the shortest distance: home to Clarksville, Clarksville to the park, or the Hiking Trail?

41. Rounding to the nearest ten, use mental math to estimate how much longer the second part of the trip is than the first.

42. How many miles is the trip from home to Clapton State Park?

43. If Kevin gets 27.5 miles per gallon of gas and his gas tank holds 14.6 gallons, how many miles does Kevin usually get on a full tank of gas?

44. Can he make the trip to Clapton State Park on one tank of gas?

45. Rounding to the nearest whole number, use mental math to estimate the cost of a tank of gas.

46. About how much money do you think Kevin should expect to spend on gas for the round trip?

47. The hikers want to complete the Hiking Trail in 3 days. Round to the nearest whole number and use mental math to estimate how many miles they should walk each day.

Order the decimals from least to greatest.

1. 2.3, 2.59, 2.09   **2.** 1.02, 1.2, 1.19   **3.** 4.001, 2.3, 2.31   **4.** .3, .07, .099

Match the decimal with the corresponding letter on the number line.

5. 2.4   **6.** 1.99   **7.** 2.22   **8.** 3   **9.** 2.60

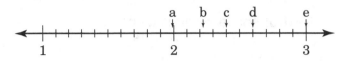

Find the sum or difference.

10. 2.68 + 2.32   **11.** 12.8 − 4.9   **12.** 1.45 + 3.9   **13.** $11.00 − $.45

14. .78 + 3.89   **15.** 4.01 − 3.45   **16.** .209 + .93   **17.** 1 − .4

18. 7.1 − 2.32   **19.** .723 + 1.277   **20.** 16 + .5   **21.** 20.01 − 3.09

Find the product or quotient.

22. 12.4 × .03   **23.** 1.5 ÷ .03   **24.** .4 × .4   **25.** 1.7 ÷ 17

26. 1.25 × .02   **27.** 54.2 ÷ .16   **28.** 4.78 × 100   **29.** 12.3 × 100

30. 16 × .25   **31.** 1.62 ÷ .03   **32.** 120 × .6   **33.** .5 ÷ 5

Solve.

34. Nicole and her friends met at her house to go in-line skating. They skated 5.7 miles, then turned around and skated 2.8 miles back toward home before Nicole's mom picked them up and drove them the rest of the way home. How many miles did they drive? How many miles did they skate?

35. If Mia can run a mile in 6.5 minutes, estimate how long it would take her to run 3 miles. Then calculate the actual time it would take her.

36. Chad's soccer team raised $94.50 selling candy bars. If each candy bar costs $1.50, how many did they sell?

37. For his Spanish club's booth at the street fair, Danny had to buy 12 pounds of tomatoes. Tomatoes cost $.69 a pound. The cost is split equally among 4 people. How much does each person pay?

Chapter 3
Adding and Subtracting Fractions and Mixed Numbers

In this chapter, you will learn

- To name and write fractions
- To rename mixed numbers as improper fractions
- To rename improper fractions as mixed numbers
- To find equivalent fractions
- To write fractions in lowest terms
- To find like fractions and compare fractions
- To add and subtract fractions with the same denominator
- To add and subtract fractions with different denominators
- To add mixed numbers
- To subtract mixed numbers

Fractions are part of everyday life. Time passes in parts of an hour, distances are measured in parts of miles, and food is often purchased in parts of pounds or prepared using parts of various measurements, such as cups or tablespoons. Take a look at this list of ingredients for a chocolate chip cookie recipe.

When you are baking, you might need to answer questions such as these: How many cups of ingredients are there all together? How much more brown sugar than white sugar is used?

In this chapter you will learn how to find the answers to these and other questions involving fractions.

Chocolate Chip Cookies
$\frac{1}{2}$ cup butter
2 eggs
$2\frac{1}{3}$ cups flour
$\frac{3}{4}$ cup brown sugar
$\frac{1}{2}$ cup white sugar
1 teaspoon baking soda
1 teaspoon vanilla extract
$\frac{2}{3}$ cup chopped nuts
$2\frac{1}{4}$ cups chocolate chips

3.1 Writing Fractions

In This Lesson, You Will Learn

To name and write fractions

Words to Learn

Fraction a number that names part of a whole

Denominator the bottom number of a fraction

Numerator the top number of a fraction

David had a party for his friend Chang's birthday. After the party the following food items were left over.

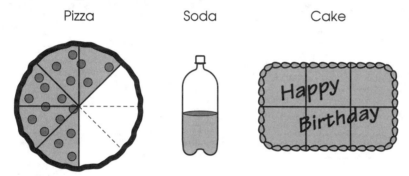

Pizza   Soda   Cake

New Idea

To describe the food items left, David uses fractions. **Fractions** are numbers that describe equal parts of a whole. A fraction is made up of 2 numbers. The bottom number is the **denominator.** It is the number of equal parts in the whole. The top number is the **numerator.** It is the number of parts of the whole that are being counted.

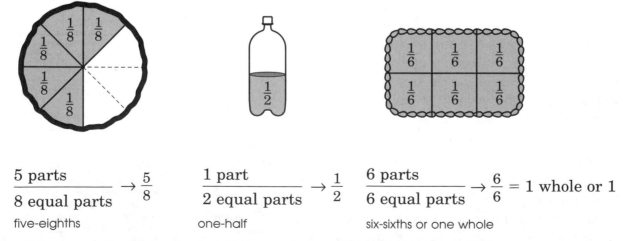

$$\frac{5 \text{ parts}}{8 \text{ equal parts}} \rightarrow \frac{5}{8}$$

five-eighths

$$\frac{1 \text{ part}}{2 \text{ equal parts}} \rightarrow \frac{1}{2}$$

one-half

$$\frac{6 \text{ parts}}{6 \text{ equal parts}} \rightarrow \frac{6}{6} = 1 \text{ whole or } 1$$

six-sixths or one whole

Fractions can also show parts of a group, as well as parts of a whole.

Example 1: There were 7 bags of popcorn for the party. 4 of them had butter. Name the fraction of bags of buttered popcorn.

$$\frac{\text{Bags of buttered popcorn}}{\text{Bags of popcorn}} = \frac{4}{7}$$

$\frac{4}{7}$ of the popcorn was buttered.

Example 2: There were 15 people at the party. 8 were from the city. Name the fraction of people from the city.

$$\frac{\text{People from the city}}{\text{People at the party}} = \frac{8}{15}$$

$\frac{8}{15}$ of the people at the party were from the city.

Focus on the Idea

Fractions count equal parts of a whole. The numerator shows how many parts of the whole are being counted. The denominator shows the number of equal parts in the whole. When the numerator and the denominator are the same, the fraction is equal to 1 whole.

Practice *Show your work on a separate sheet of paper.*

What fraction of each figure is shaded?

1.

2.

3.

4.

5.

6.

7.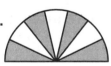

8.

Apply the Idea

A pizza has 8 slices. David ate 3 and Chang ate 5.

9. Draw a picture that shows what fraction of the pizza David ate.

10. Draw a picture that shows what fraction of the pizza Chang ate.

Write About It

11. Does this picture show $\frac{1}{3}$? Explain your answer.

3.2 Renaming Mixed Numbers and Improper Fractions

In This Lesson, You Will Learn
To rename mixed numbers as improper fractions
To rename improper fractions as mixed numbers

Words to Learn
Mixed number a number written with a whole number and a fraction

Improper fraction a fraction in which the numerator is larger than the denominator

Karin wants to do some baking over the weekend. She finds $2\frac{1}{4}$ pounds of butter in the freezer. Each pound of butter is divided into 4 sticks that weigh $\frac{1}{4}$ pound each. Most of the recipes she plans to make need $\frac{1}{4}$ pound of butter. How can she rewrite $2\frac{1}{4}$ to show how many $\frac{1}{4}$-pound sticks of butter she has?

New Idea
The number $2\frac{1}{4}$, read "two and one-fourth," is a **mixed number**. It is made up of a whole number and a fraction.

To find out how many $\frac{1}{4}$s there are in $2\frac{1}{4}$, write the two wholes as fourths. When you count the number of fourths in the picture, you can see there are 9 fourths all together, so $2\frac{1}{4} = \frac{9}{4}$. The fraction $\frac{9}{4}$ is called an **improper fraction** because the numerator is larger than the denominator.

To change a mixed number to an improper fraction, multiply the whole number by the denominator. Then add the numerator to this product. The number you get becomes the new numerator. Keep the same denominator.

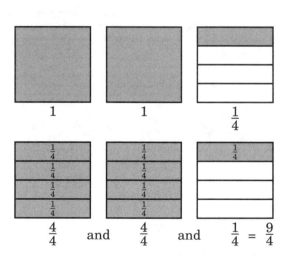

Example: Write $3\frac{1}{2}$ as an improper fraction.

Step 1: Multiply the whole number by the denominator.

$3\frac{1}{2}$ $3 \times 2 = 6$

Step 2: Add the numerator to the product. Make this the new numerator. Keep the denominator the same.

$$3\frac{1}{2} = \frac{7}{2}$$

$$\frac{6+1}{2} = \frac{7}{2}$$

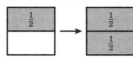

You also can change an improper fraction to a mixed number. Divide the numerator by the denominator to find the number of wholes. The remainder, the number of parts left over, is written as a fraction with the same denominator as the original improper fraction.

Example: Write $\frac{16}{3}$ as a mixed number.

Step 1: Divide the numerator by the denominator.

Step 2: Write the remainder as a fraction of the denominator.

$$\frac{16}{3} = 5\frac{1}{3}$$

$$\begin{array}{r} 5 \\ 3\overline{)16} \\ \underline{15} \\ 1 \end{array}$$

$5\frac{1}{3}$ ← remainder
← denominator

Focus on the Idea

To write a mixed number as an improper fraction, multiply the whole number by the denominator of the fraction. Add the product to the numerator. Keep the denominator the same. To write an improper fraction as a mixed number, divide the numerator by the denominator. Write the remainder as a fraction of the denominator.

Practice *Show your work on a separate sheet of paper.*

Write each improper fraction as a mixed number or a whole number.

1. $\frac{13}{8}$ 2. $\frac{10}{3}$ 3. $\frac{9}{2}$ 4. $\frac{11}{4}$ 5. $\frac{9}{3}$

Write each mixed number as an improper fraction.

6. $3\frac{1}{4}$ 7. $4\frac{3}{4}$ 8. $6\frac{1}{2}$ 9. $1\frac{3}{8}$ 10. $2\frac{5}{6}$

Apply the Idea

11. James is installing tiles that are $\frac{1}{3}$ foot long. He is covering a hall floor that measures $8\frac{2}{3}$ feet long. Write $8\frac{2}{3}$ as an improper fraction to show how many tiles he needs to complete one row.

Write About It

12. Is it easier to use an improper fraction than a mixed number? Explain.

3.3 Finding Equivalent Fractions

In This Lesson, You Will Learn
To find equivalent fractions

Words to Learn
Equivalent fractions fractions that name the same amount

Michelle is making her own dress for the junior prom. The pattern she is following says that she should sew the seams $\frac{3}{4}$ inch from the edge of the fabric. But Michelle is using a ruler that is marked in $\frac{1}{8}$ inches. How can she find out how many $\frac{1}{8}$ inches are equal to $\frac{3}{4}$ inch?

New Idea
Michelle needs to find the number of eighths that will give her a fraction with the same value as $\frac{3}{4}$. Fractions that use different numbers but name the same amount are called **equivalent fractions**.

When she looks closely at the ruler, she discovers that $\frac{6}{8}$ inch is the same as $\frac{3}{4}$ inch.

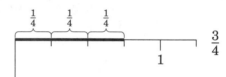

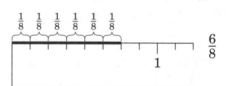

$$\frac{3}{4} = \frac{6}{8} \leftarrow \frac{3 \times 2}{4 \times 2}$$

You can find equivalent fractions by multiplying the numerator and denominator of a fraction by the same number.

Example: Multiply the numerator and denominator of $\frac{2}{3}$ by 2 and then by 3 to find two fractions equivalent to $\frac{2}{3}$.

$$\frac{2}{3}$$

$$\frac{2}{3} \times \frac{2}{2} = \frac{4}{6}$$

$$\frac{2}{3} \times \frac{3}{3} = \frac{6}{9}$$

These are all equivalent fractions.

$$\frac{2}{3} = \frac{4}{6} = \frac{6}{9}$$

✓ Check Your Understanding

Find 6 equivalent fractions to complete the pattern.

$$\frac{1}{2} = \frac{2}{4} = \frac{3}{6} =$$

Focus on the Idea

To find equivalent fractions, multiply the numerator and denominator by the same number.

Practice *Show your work on a separate sheet of paper.*

Find an equivalent fraction for each fraction below by multiplying the numerator and denominator by 3.

1. $\frac{3}{8}$
2. $\frac{2}{7}$
3. $\frac{3}{4}$
4. $\frac{5}{6}$
5. $\frac{3}{3}$

Find an equivalent fraction for each fraction below by multiplying the numerator and denominator by 4.

6. $\frac{3}{5}$
7. $\frac{2}{5}$
8. $\frac{1}{4}$
9. $\frac{2}{2}$
10. $\frac{2}{9}$

Extend the Idea

Sometimes it is necessary to find a missing numerator or denominator to find an equivalent fraction. You can find the missing number using division and multiplication.

Example 1: Find an equivalent fraction of $\frac{3}{5}$ with a denominator of 10.

Step 1: Set up the fraction parts you know.

$$\frac{3}{5} = \frac{?}{10}$$

Step 2: Divide the numerators or the denominators. Because you have both denominators, divide the denominators.

$$10 \div 5 = 2$$

Step 3: Because the new denominator is *larger* than the first denominator, *multiply* the known numerator by the quotient.

$$3 \times 2 = 6$$

$$\frac{3}{5} = \frac{6}{10}$$

Step 4: To check your answer, make sure you can either multiply or divide the numerator and denominator of the original fraction by the same number to find the new fraction.

$$\overset{\times 2}{\underset{\times 2}{\frac{3}{5} = \frac{6}{10}}}$$

$\frac{3}{5}$ is equivalent to $\frac{6}{10}$.

Example 2: Find an equivalent fraction of $\frac{8}{12}$ with a denominator of 3.

Step 1: Set up the fraction parts you know.

$$\frac{8}{12} = \frac{?}{3}$$

Step 2: Divide the numerators or the denominators. Because you have both denominators, divide the denominators.

$$12 \div 3 = 4$$

Step 3: Because the new denominator is *smaller* than the first, *divide* the known numerator by the quotient.

$$8 \div 4 = 2$$

$$\frac{8}{12} = \frac{2}{3}$$

Step 4: To check your answer, make sure you can either multiply or divide the numerator and denominator of the original fraction by the same number to find the new fraction.

$$\frac{8}{12} = \frac{2}{3}$$

(÷ 4 ... ÷ 4)

$\frac{8}{12}$ is equivalent to $\frac{2}{3}$.

Example 3: Find an equivalent fraction of $\frac{3}{5}$ with a numerator of 18.

Step 1: Set up the fraction parts you know.

$$\frac{3}{5} = \frac{18}{?}$$

Step 2: Divide the numerators or the denominators. Because you have both numerators, divide the numerators.

$$18 \div 3 = 6$$

Step 3: Because the new numerator is *larger* than the first numerator, *multiply* the known denominator by the quotient.

$$5 \times 6 = 30$$

$$\frac{3}{5} = \frac{18}{30}$$

Step 4: To check your answer, make sure you can either multiply or divide the numerator and denominator of the original fraction by the same number to find the new fraction.

$$\frac{3}{5} = \frac{18}{30}$$

(× 6 ... × 6)

$\frac{3}{5}$ is equivalent to $\frac{18}{30}$.

✓ Check the Math

Look at the two fractions below:

$\frac{5}{11}$ and $\frac{7}{13}$

What are some of the ways you can tell that they are not equivalent fractions?

Practice *Show your work on a separate sheet of paper.*

Find the missing numerator or denominator to write equivalent fractions.

11. $\frac{3}{4} = \frac{?}{12}$ 12. $\frac{6}{?} = \frac{36}{42}$ 13. $\frac{?}{30} = \frac{2}{3}$ 14. $\frac{1}{2} = \frac{12}{?}$

15. $\frac{?}{10} = \frac{18}{20}$ 16. $\frac{2}{5} = \frac{?}{10}$ 17. $\frac{3}{4} = \frac{75}{?}$ 18. $\frac{?}{100} = \frac{4}{5}$

19. $\frac{16}{?} = \frac{4}{5}$ 20. $\frac{2}{7} = \frac{20}{?}$ 21. $\frac{1}{6} = \frac{?}{48}$ 22. $\frac{3}{8} = \frac{?}{32}$

Tell whether the pairs of fractions are equivalent fractions.

23. $\frac{2}{3}$ and $\frac{3}{6}$ 24. $\frac{6}{12}$ and $\frac{1}{2}$ 25. $\frac{3}{5}$ and $\frac{3}{10}$ 26. $\frac{4}{7}$ and $\frac{12}{21}$

Apply the Idea

27. Ruth is using a ruler marked in $\frac{1}{16}$ inches. She has to measure $\frac{3}{4}$ inch. Find an equivalent fraction with 16 as the denominator.

28. Joe figures he spends $\frac{1}{3}$ of his day sleeping. Find an equivalent fraction with 24 as the denominator.

29. Megan has $\frac{2}{3}$ pound of chocolate. She has to divide it 6 ways. Find an equivalent fraction with 6 as the numerator.

✏ Write About It

30. Look at the two pictures. How much of each is shaded? Do the two pictures show equivalent fractions? Are the shaded portions equal? Explain your answers.

3.4 Writing Fractions in Lowest Terms

In This Lesson, You Will Learn
To write fractions in lowest terms

Words to Learn
Factor a whole number that divides into another number with no remainder

Lowest terms a fraction is in lowest terms when the numerator and the denominator of the fraction cannot be divided evenly by any number other than 1

Greatest common factor (GCF) the largest factor that two or more numbers share

---

Joanna spends 6 hours of each weekday at school. As a fraction of a 24-hour day, Joanna spends $\frac{6}{24}$ of her time in school. How can she rewrite $\frac{6}{24}$ as an equivalent fraction that is easier to understand and work with?

New Idea
By looking at the two circles, you can see that $\frac{6}{24}$ is equal to $\frac{1}{4}$.

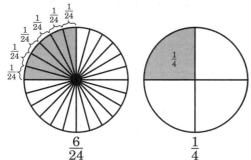

$$\frac{6}{24} = \frac{1}{4} \quad \begin{matrix} \leftarrow \\ \leftarrow \end{matrix} \quad \frac{6 \div 6}{24 \div 6}$$

When you divide the numerator and denominator by the same number, you get an equivalent fraction in lower terms. To write a fraction in lower terms, look for factors of both the numerator and denominator. A **factor** of a number is a whole number that divides evenly into that number.

Look at the factors of 18. Notice that six numbers divide evenly into 18.

$$18 \div 1 = 18 \qquad 18 \div 2 = 9 \qquad 18 \div 3 = 6$$

$$18 \div 6 = 3 \qquad 18 \div 9 = 2 \qquad 18 \div 18 = 1$$

The factors of 18 are 1, 2, 3, 6, 9, and 18.

1 and the number itself are always factors of a number. You can find the other factors by dividing by whole numbers. Start by dividing the number by 2. The quotient tells you the highest possible value of the remaining factors.

Example 1: Find the factors of 12.
1 and 12 are factors.
$12 \div 2 = 6 \quad \rightarrow \quad$ 2 and 6 are factors.
$\qquad\qquad\qquad\qquad$ All other factors are less than 6.
$12 \div 3 = 4 \quad \rightarrow \quad$ 3 and 4 are factors.
$12 \div 5 = 2 \text{ R}2 \rightarrow$ 5 is not a factor.
Stop. 6 is next, you already know that it is a factor.

The factors of 12 are 1, 2, 3, 4, 6, and 12.

Example 2: Find the factors of 11.
1 and 11 are factors.
$11 \div 2 = 5 \text{ R}1 \rightarrow$ 2 and 5 are not factors.
$\qquad\qquad\qquad\qquad$ All other factors are less than 5.
$11 \div 3 = 3 \text{ R}2 \rightarrow$ 3 is not a factor.
$11 \div 4 = 2 \text{ R}3 \rightarrow$ 4 is not a factor.

Stop. You already know that 5 is not a factor. The only factors of 11 are 1 and 11.

A fraction is in **lowest terms** when 1 is the only number that divides evenly into the numerator and denominator. Sometimes writing a fraction in lowest terms is called *reducing* a fraction or *simplifying* a fraction.

Example 1: Write $\dfrac{9}{15}$ in lowest terms.

Step 1: Look for a factor of both the numerator (9) and the denominator (15). 3 divides evenly into 9 and 15. Divide the numerator and denominator by 3.
$$\frac{9 \div 3}{15 \div 3} = \frac{3}{5}$$

Step 2: Look for a factor of both 3 and 5. 1 is the only number that divides evenly into both 3 and 5, so the fraction must be in lowest terms.
$$\frac{3}{5}$$

$$\frac{9}{15} = \frac{3}{5}$$

Example 2: Write $\dfrac{8}{24}$ in lowest terms.

Step 1: Look for a factor of both the numerator (8) and the denominator (24). 2 divides evenly into 8 and 24. Divide the numerator and denominator by 2.
$$\frac{8 \div 2}{24 \div 2} = \frac{4}{12}$$

Step 2: Look for a factor of both 4 and 12. 4 divides evenly into 4 and 12. Divide the numerator and denominator by 4. 1 is the only factor that divides evenly into both 1 and 3, so the fraction must be in lowest terms.

$$\frac{4 \div 4}{12 \div 4} = \frac{1}{3}$$

$$\frac{8}{24} = \frac{1}{3}$$

Focus on the Idea

To write a fraction in lowest terms, divide the numerator and denominator by the same number. Continue dividing by factors until 1 is the only number that will divide evenly into both the numerator and denominator.

Practice *Show your work on a separate sheet of paper.*

Find the factors of each number.

1. 4   **2.** 13   **3.** 20   **4.** 36

Choose the fraction from each pair that is in lowest terms.

5. $\frac{2}{3}$ $\frac{4}{8}$ **6.** $\frac{3}{6}$ $\frac{3}{7}$ **7.** $\frac{8}{24}$ $\frac{7}{32}$

8. $\frac{6}{15}$ $\frac{5}{12}$ **9.** $\frac{9}{12}$ $\frac{11}{15}$ **10.** $\frac{3}{4}$ $\frac{3}{9}$

Write each fraction in lowest terms.

11. $\frac{6}{8}$ **12.** $\frac{8}{16}$ **13.** $\frac{10}{15}$ **14.** $\frac{40}{75}$ **15.** $\frac{10}{30}$

16. $\frac{16}{44}$ **17.** $\frac{35}{40}$ **18.** $\frac{33}{77}$ **19.** $\frac{18}{24}$ **20.** $\frac{24}{48}$

Extend the Idea

You can write a fraction in lowest terms in fewer steps. First find the largest factor the numerator and denominator share. This is their **greatest common factor (GCF)**. Then divide the numerator and denominator by the GCF.

Example 1: Write $\frac{4}{12}$ in lowest terms.

Step 1: List the factors of the numerator (4) and denominator (12). 4 is the greatest common factor.

4: 1, 2, 4

12: 1, 2, 3, 4, 6, 12

Step 2: Divide the numerator and denominator by the greatest common factor (4).

$$\frac{4}{12} = \frac{1}{3}$$

$$\frac{4 \div 4}{12 \div 4} = \frac{1}{3}$$

Example 2: Write $\frac{18}{24}$ in lowest terms.

Step 1: List the factors of the numerator (18) and denominator (24). 6 is the greatest common factor.

18: 1, 2, 3, 6, 9, 18

24: 1, 2, 3, 4, 6, 8, 12, 24

Step 2: Divide the numerator and denominator by the greatest common factor (6).

$$\frac{18}{24} = \frac{3}{4}$$

$$\frac{18 \div 6}{24 \div 6} = \frac{3}{4}$$

✓ Check the Math

Joanna wrote $\frac{16}{24}$ in lowest terms as $\frac{8}{12}$. Is she correct? What was her mistake?

Practice *Show your work on a separate sheet of paper.*

Find the factors and the greatest common factor for each pair of numbers.

21. 15 and 9   **22.** 12 and 16   **23.** 6 and 18

24. 18 and 24   **25.** 36 and 48   **26.** 12 and 35

Apply the Idea

Write each fraction in lowest terms.

27. What fraction of a year is 4 months?

28. What fraction of a day is 3 hours?

29. What fraction of an hour is 15 minutes?

30. What fraction of an hour is 20 minutes?

31. What fraction of a dollar is 25 cents?

32. What fraction of a dollar is 20 cents?

✏️ Write About It

33. Why do you think it is a good idea to work with fractions reduced to their lowest terms? When might you want to leave a fraction in its original form instead of reducing it to lowest terms?

3.5 Comparing Fractions

In This Lesson, You Will Learn
To find like fractions
To compare fractions

Words to Learn
Like fractions fractions with the same denominators

Multiple of a number the product of the number and a whole number

Common multiple a number that is a multiple of two or more different numbers

Common denominator a common multiple of two or more denominators

---

Kareem returns bottles for his neighbors. One neighbor says he can keep $\frac{1}{6}$ of the deposit money from his bottles, another says he can keep $\frac{3}{4}$, and the third says he can keep $\frac{5}{6}$. How can Kareem tell who will give him the largest part of his or her bottle money?

New Idea
Kareem needs to compare fractions to find the largest fraction. $\frac{1}{6}$ and $\frac{5}{6}$ are **like fractions** because they have the same denominator. It is easy to compare like fractions by looking at their numerators.

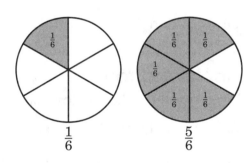

5 is larger than 1.
$\frac{5}{6}$ is larger than $\frac{1}{6}$.

When comparing fractions with different denominators you must first change them to like fractions. To do this, you must find equivalent fractions with the same denominators. Begin by finding common multiples of the denominators. You find **multiples of a number** by multiplying the number by whole numbers. When two or more numbers share the same multiple, that multiple is called a **common multiple**. A common multiple of two or more denominators is called a **common denominator**.

Example: Compare $\frac{3}{4}$ and $\frac{5}{6}$.

Step 1: List the multiples of each denominator. 12 is the smallest multiple other than zero that is the same for both.

multiples of 4: 0, 4, 8, 12, . . .

multiples of 6: 0, 6, 12, . . .

Step 2: Find equivalent fractions with 12 as the denominator. Divide the 12 by each original denominator. Multiply both the numerator and original denominator by the quotient.

$$12 \div 4 = 3$$

$$\frac{3}{4} = \frac{3 \times 3}{4 \times 3} = \frac{9}{12}$$

$$12 \div 6 = 2$$

$$\frac{5}{6} = \frac{5 \times 2}{6 \times 2} = \frac{10}{12}$$

Step 3: Compare the numerators. $\frac{5}{6}$ is greater than $\frac{3}{4}$.

$$10 > 9, \text{ so } \frac{10}{12} > \frac{9}{12}$$

A simple way to find a common multiple is to multiply the denominators.

Example: Find like fractions for $\frac{6}{11}$ and $\frac{7}{13}$.

Step 1: Multiply the denominators. Use 143 as the common denominator.

$$11 \times 13 = 143$$

Step 2: Find equivalent fractions.

$$\frac{6}{11} = \frac{6 \times 13}{11 \times 13} = \frac{78}{143} \qquad \frac{7}{13} = \frac{7 \times 11}{13 \times 11} = \frac{77}{143}$$

Focus on the Idea

To compare like fractions, compare the numerators. To compare fractions with different denominators, first find a common multiple of the denominators. Then use the common multiple to find equivalent fractions. Then compare the numerators to find which is greater.

Practice *Show your work on a separate sheet of paper.*

Compare the fraction pairs. Name the larger of each pair.

1. $\frac{4}{5}, \frac{3}{15}$ 2. $\frac{2}{3}, \frac{4}{8}$ 3. $\frac{1}{5}, \frac{9}{27}$ 4. $\frac{4}{6}, \frac{1}{3}$ 5. $\frac{1}{8}, \frac{3}{24}$ 6. $\frac{2}{3}, \frac{3}{5}$

Apply the Idea

7. Each year Jen sets goals for herself. Last year she met $\frac{2}{3}$ of her goals. This year she met $\frac{7}{12}$ of her goals. In which year did she meet more of her goals?

Write About It

8. Explain how you might be able to tell that $\frac{1}{4}$ is bigger than $\frac{1}{5}$ without finding like fractions.

3.6 Adding and Subtracting Like Fractions

In This Lesson, You Will Learn

To add fractions with the same denominator

To subtract fractions with the same denominator

Words to Learn

Like fractions fractions with the same denominators

After school, Emily and Andrea sometimes stop at the deli for a sandwich. This time they ordered a foot-long hero sandwich. The server cut the sandwich into fifths. Emily ate $\frac{2}{5}$ and Andrea ate $\frac{1}{5}$. How much of the sandwich did they eat together?

New Idea

To find out how much Emily and Andrea ate, you must add fractions. Fractions whose denominators are the same, such as $\frac{2}{5}$ and $\frac{1}{5}$, are called **like fractions**. To add like fractions, add only the numerators; the denominator stays the same. If the answer is an improper fraction, write it as a mixed number. Write all fractions in lowest terms.

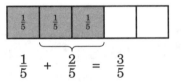

$$\frac{1}{5} + \frac{2}{5} = \frac{3}{5}$$

Example: Add $\frac{3}{8} + \frac{7}{8}$.

Step 1: Add the numerators.

Keep the denominator the same.

$$\frac{3+7}{8} = \frac{10}{8}$$

Step 2: Change the improper fraction to a mixed number.

$$\frac{10}{8} = 1\frac{2}{8}$$

Step 3: Write the fraction in lowest terms. 2 is the greatest common factor of 2 and 8. Divide the numerator and denominator by 2.

$$\frac{2}{8} = \frac{2 \div 2}{8 \div 2} = \frac{1}{4}$$

The sum of $\frac{3}{8}$ and $\frac{7}{8}$ is $1\frac{1}{4}$.

To find out how much is left of the sandwich Emily and Andrea were eating, you need to subtract $\frac{3}{5}$ from the whole. Write the whole, or 1, as the like fraction $\frac{5}{5}$. To subtract like fractions, subtract the numerators and keep the denominator the same. Write the answer in lowest terms.

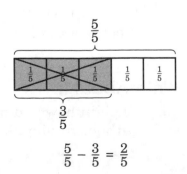

$$\frac{5}{5} - \frac{3}{5} = \frac{2}{5}$$

Example: Subtract $\dfrac{7}{12} - \dfrac{3}{12}$.

Step 1: Subtract the numerators. Keep the denominator the same.

$$\dfrac{7-3}{12} = \dfrac{4}{12}$$

Step 2: Write the fraction in lowest terms. The greatest common factor of 4 and 12 is 4. Divide the numerator and denominator by 4.

$$\dfrac{4 \div 4}{12 \div 4} = \dfrac{1}{3}$$

$$\dfrac{7}{12} - \dfrac{3}{12} = \dfrac{4}{12} = \dfrac{1}{3}$$

Focus on the Idea

To add or subtract like fractions, add or subtract the numerators. Keep the denominators the same. Write improper fractions as mixed numbers and write the answer in lowest terms.

Practice *Show your work on a separate sheet of paper.*

Add. Write the answer in lowest terms.

1. $\dfrac{2}{5} + \dfrac{1}{5}$ 2. $\dfrac{3}{7} + \dfrac{3}{7}$ 3. $\dfrac{3}{10} + \dfrac{2}{10}$ 4. $\dfrac{1}{2} + \dfrac{1}{2}$

5. $\dfrac{11}{14} + \dfrac{3}{14}$ 6. $\dfrac{5}{12} + \dfrac{3}{12}$ 7. $\dfrac{4}{13} + \dfrac{5}{13}$ 8. $\dfrac{3}{16} + \dfrac{5}{16}$

Subtract. Write the answer in lowest terms.

9. $\dfrac{4}{5} - \dfrac{1}{5}$ 10. $\dfrac{11}{15} - \dfrac{2}{15}$ 11. $\dfrac{8}{9} - \dfrac{8}{9}$ 12. $1 - \dfrac{1}{3}$

13. $\dfrac{10}{12} - \dfrac{8}{12}$ 14. $\dfrac{18}{20} - \dfrac{4}{20}$ 15. $1 - \dfrac{3}{4}$ 16. $\dfrac{8}{25} - \dfrac{3}{25}$

Apply the Idea

17. To make money after school, Emily delivers evening papers. Her route takes her $\dfrac{3}{10}$ mile south of her house, then $\dfrac{2}{10}$ mile east, and finally $\dfrac{4}{10}$ mile back home. What is the total distance Emily covers?

18. Emily is saving $\dfrac{3}{4}$ of the money she earns to buy a computer. What fraction of her money does she have left to spend on other things? (Hint: All of her money is $\dfrac{4}{4}$.)

Write About It

19. Describe a situation in real life where you would need to add or subtract like fractions. Make up a problem based on that situation.

3.7 Adding and Subtracting Unlike Fractions

In This Lesson, You Will Learn
To add fractions with different denominators
To subtract fractions with different denominators

Words to Learn
Unlike fractions fractions with different denominators

Maria is a member of the track team. During practice one afternoon, she sprints $\frac{1}{4}$ mile and then jogs for $\frac{1}{8}$ mile. What is the total distance she runs?

New Idea

To find the total you need to add the fractions $\frac{1}{4}$ and $\frac{1}{8}$. These are **unlike fractions** because they have different denominators. You cannot add unlike fractions the way you add like fractions. You must first change the unlike fractions to equivalent fractions with a common denominator.

$$\frac{1}{4} + \frac{1}{8} = \frac{2}{8} + \frac{1}{8} = \frac{3}{8}$$

Example: Add $\frac{5}{6} + \frac{3}{4}$.

Step 1: Find a common denominator. List the multiples of 6 and 4.

4: 0, 4, 8, 12
6: 0, 6, 12

Step 2: Find equivalent fractions with the common denominator.

$12 \div 6 = 2$

$$\frac{5}{6} = \frac{5 \times 2}{6 \times 2} = \frac{10}{12}$$

$12 \div 4 = 3$

$$\frac{3}{4} = \frac{3 \times 3}{4 \times 3} = \frac{9}{12}$$

Step 3: Add the like fractions.

$$\frac{10}{12} + \frac{9}{12} = \frac{19}{12}$$

Step 4: Write the improper fraction as a mixed number.

$$\frac{19}{12} = 1\frac{7}{12}$$

$$\frac{5}{6} + \frac{3}{4} = \frac{19}{12} = 1\frac{7}{12}$$

Subtract unlike fractions the same way.

Example: Subtract $\frac{4}{5} - \frac{1}{10}$.

    Step 1: Find a common denominator.   5: 0, 5, 10
                List the multiples of 5 and 10.   10: 0, 10

    Step 2: Find equivalent fractions with the $10 \div 5 = 2$
                common denominator.

                $\frac{1}{10}$ does not change. $\frac{4}{5} = \frac{4 \times 2}{5 \times 2} = \frac{8}{10}$

    Step 3: Subtract the like fractions. $\frac{8}{10} - \frac{1}{10} = \frac{7}{10}$

              $\frac{4}{5} - \frac{1}{10} = \frac{7}{10}$

Focus on the Idea

To add or subtract unlike fractions, find a common denominator and make equivalent like fractions. Then add or subtract the numerators and keep the denominators the same. Write the answer in lowest terms.

Practice *Show your work on a separate sheet of paper.*

Add. Write the answer in lowest terms.

1. $\frac{1}{6} + \frac{1}{3}$ 2. $\frac{3}{4} + \frac{1}{5}$ 3. $\frac{1}{10} + \frac{2}{5}$ 4. $\frac{1}{2} + \frac{1}{3}$

5. $\frac{1}{10} + \frac{5}{6}$ 6. $\frac{3}{4} + \frac{2}{3}$ 7. $\frac{3}{8} + \frac{1}{5}$ 8. $\frac{4}{9} + \frac{1}{6}$

Subtract. Write the answer in lowest terms.

9. $\frac{3}{5} - \frac{9}{20}$ 10. $\frac{1}{3} - \frac{1}{4}$ 11. $\frac{3}{4} - \frac{2}{3}$ 12. $\frac{7}{8} - \frac{5}{12}$

13. $\frac{1}{2} - \frac{1}{3}$ 14. $\frac{7}{8} - \frac{3}{4}$ 15. $\frac{9}{10} - \frac{2}{3}$ 16. $\frac{3}{4} - \frac{7}{10}$

Apply the Idea

17. The track coach raised the high jump bar $\frac{1}{2}$ inch and then $\frac{3}{4}$ inch during practice. How much did he raise it all together?

18. Maria's coach has her run $\frac{3}{4}$ mile, sprint $\frac{1}{2}$ mile, and then jog $\frac{1}{8}$ mile. How far does Maria go in all?

Write About It

19. Explain the steps you would take to add $\frac{3}{7}$ and $\frac{1}{5}$.

⬇ 3.8 Adding Mixed Numbers

In This Lesson, You Will Learn

To add mixed numbers

Gary's parents add $1 to his weekly allowance for every hour he spends tutoring his younger brother. He tutored for $1\frac{3}{4}$ hours on Thursday and $2\frac{3}{4}$ hours on Saturday. How much time did he spend tutoring?

New Idea

To find the total time, Gary needs to add the mixed numbers $1\frac{3}{4}$ and $2\frac{3}{4}$. He rearranges the numbers so that he adds the whole numbers and then the fractions.

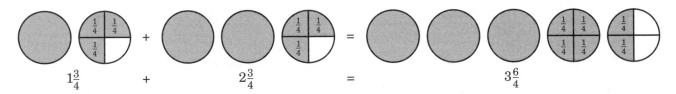

Gary has 3 whole hours and $\frac{6}{4}$ hours. He then renames $\frac{6}{4}$ as $1\frac{1}{2}$.

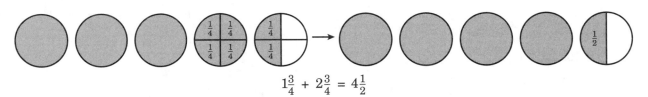

$$1\frac{3}{4} + 2\frac{3}{4} = 4\frac{1}{2}$$

Gary spent $4\frac{1}{2}$ hours tutoring.

To add mixed numbers, add the whole numbers and then add the fractions. If the fractions are unlike, start by changing them to equivalent fractions with the same denominators. After you have added, rename an improper fraction in the sum as a mixed number and then add to the whole number.

Example: Add $2\frac{1}{4} + 3\frac{4}{5}$.

   Step 1: Start by changing $\frac{1}{4}$ and $\frac{4}{5}$ to like fractions.

   Find a common denominator.   4: 0, 4, 8, 12, 16, 20
   List the multiples of 4 and 5.   5: 0, 5, 10, 15, 20

Step 2: Make equivalent fractions for $\frac{1}{4}$ and $\frac{4}{5}$.

$$20 \div 4 = 5$$
$$\frac{1}{4} = \frac{1 \times 5}{4 \times 5} = \frac{5}{20}$$

$$20 \div 5 = 4$$
$$\frac{4}{5} = \frac{4 \times 4}{5 \times 4} = \frac{16}{20}$$

Step 3: Rewrite the problem and add the whole numbers and like fractions.

$$\begin{array}{r} 2\frac{1}{4} = 2\frac{5}{20} \\ +\,3\frac{4}{5} = 3\frac{16}{20} \\ \hline 5\frac{21}{20} \end{array}$$

Step 4: Rename the improper fraction as a mixed number.

$$5\frac{21}{20}$$
$$5 + 1\frac{1}{20}$$
$$6\frac{1}{20}$$

$$2\frac{1}{4} + 3\frac{4}{5} = 6\frac{1}{20}$$

Focus on the Idea

To add mixed numbers, find equivalent like fractions. Add the whole numbers and then add the fractions. Rename an improper fraction in the sum as a mixed number and add to the whole number. Write the answer in lowest terms.

Practice *Show your work on a separate sheet of paper.*

Add. Write the answer in lowest terms.

1. $2\frac{1}{9} + 3\frac{4}{9}$ 2. $3\frac{5}{6} + 1\frac{2}{6}$ 3. $6\frac{3}{4} + 3\frac{2}{5}$ 4. $4 + 3\frac{1}{2}$

5. $15\frac{3}{4} + 4\frac{3}{4}$ 6. $10\frac{4}{7} + 5\frac{3}{7}$ 7. $18\frac{1}{2} + 1\frac{1}{2}$ 8. $2\frac{3}{10} + 3\frac{2}{5}$

Apply the Idea

Clyde is a member of a club that picks up trash on beaches. The chart records how many miles of beach his club cleaned in one weekend. Use the chart to answer Problem 9.

9. How many miles does the club clean:
   a. On Friday and Saturday?
   b. On Friday and Sunday?
   c. On Saturday and Sunday?
   d. In all 3 days?

Day	Miles
Friday	$3\frac{1}{2}$ miles
Saturday	$4\frac{1}{4}$ miles
Sunday	$3\frac{3}{8}$ miles

Write About It

10. Draw a picture that shows how to add $3\frac{1}{2}$ and $2\frac{3}{4}$.

3.9 Subtracting Mixed Numbers

In This Lesson, You Will Learn

To subtract mixed numbers

Rosalie is sewing a trim to the bottom edge of a school banner. If she has 6 feet of trim and the banner is $4\frac{3}{8}$ feet long, how much trim will she have left over?

New Idea

To find out how much trim is left, Rosalie has to subtract mixed numbers. Subtracting mixed numbers is much like adding mixed numbers, except you start by subtracting the fractions and then subtract the whole numbers.

In $6 - 4\frac{3}{8}$, there are no eighths to subtract from. You have to rename 6 to show more eighths.

$6 - 4\frac{3}{8} = 1\frac{5}{8}$, so there is $1\frac{5}{8}$ feet of trim left over.

To subtract mixed numbers, subtract the fractions and then subtract the whole numbers. Regroup a whole number if you cannot subtract the fractions.

Example: Subtract $5\frac{1}{2} - 2\frac{3}{4}$.

Step 1: Start by changing the fractions to like fractions. Find a common denominator for $\frac{1}{2}$ and $\frac{3}{4}$. List the multiples of 2 and 4.

2: 0, 2, 4

4: 0, 4

Step 2: Find equivalent like fractions with 4 as the denominator.

$\frac{3}{4}$ stays the same.

$4 \div 2 = 2$

$\frac{1}{2} = \frac{1 \times 2}{2 \times 2} = \frac{2}{4}$

Step 3: Rewrite the problem.

$5\frac{1}{2} - 2\frac{3}{4} = 5\frac{2}{4} - 2\frac{3}{4}$

Step 4: You cannot subtract $\frac{3}{4}$ from $\frac{2}{4}$. Regroup $5\frac{2}{4}$ to show more fourths.

$5\frac{2}{4} = 4 + 1 + \frac{2}{4}$

$4 + \frac{4}{4} + \frac{2}{4}$

$4\frac{6}{4}$

Step 5: Subtract.

$$4\frac{6}{4}$$
$$-2\frac{3}{4}$$
$$\overline{2\frac{3}{4}}$$

$$5\frac{1}{2} - 2\frac{3}{4} = 2\frac{3}{4}$$

Focus on the Idea

To subtract mixed numbers, find equivalent like fractions. Subtract the fractions and then subtract the whole numbers. If you cannot subtract the fractions, rename the whole number to show a larger fraction. Write the answer in lowest terms.

Practice *Show your work on a separate sheet of paper.*

Subtract. Write the answer in lowest terms.

1. $9\frac{3}{4} - 2\frac{1}{4}$ 2. $10 - \frac{2}{3}$ 3. $7\frac{2}{9} - 3\frac{5}{9}$ 4. $3\frac{1}{8} - \frac{5}{8}$

5. $7\frac{2}{5} - 3\frac{1}{10}$ 6. $6\frac{1}{5} - 3\frac{3}{4}$ 7. $15 - 3\frac{2}{3}$ 8. $8\frac{1}{6} - 3\frac{2}{9}$

9. $2\frac{1}{4} - 1$ 10. $7\frac{5}{8} - 3\frac{4}{5}$ 11. $6\frac{1}{2} - \frac{7}{12}$ 12. $4\frac{1}{3} - 3\frac{5}{6}$

Apply the Idea

Ernie and his band are recording songs for a demo tape. The chart below shows the length of each song. Use the chart to answer Problems 13 and 14.

13. **a.** How much longer is "Dangerous Times" than "All That"?

    b. What is the difference between the lengths of "Cool Runnin'" and "No Such Thing"?

14. Ernie is recording all the songs on a $\frac{1}{4}$-hour cassette tape. Will all the songs fit on a single tape? Explain your answer.

Song Title	Time in Minutes
Dangerous Times	$3\frac{2}{3}$
All That	$3\frac{1}{6}$
Cool Runnin'	$4\frac{5}{6}$
No Such Thing	$3\frac{1}{4}$
So Fine	$4\frac{1}{2}$

Write About It

15. Think of a situation in which you would need to add or subtract mixed numbers in real life. Write a problem that uses adding or subtracting mixed numbers.

In this chapter, you have learned

- To name and write fractions
- To rename mixed numbers as improper fractions
- To rename improper fractions as mixed numbers
- To find equivalent fractions
- To write fractions in lowest terms
- To find like fractions and compare fractions
- To add and subtract fractions with the same denominator
- To add and subtract fractions with different denominators
- To add mixed numbers
- To subtract mixed numbers

Words You Know

From the lists of Words to Learn, choose the word or phrase that best completes each statement.

1. A number that names a part of a whole is a ___.

2. ___ are fractions with the same denominators.

3. A fraction is in ___ when 1 is the only common factor of the numerator and denominator.

4. An ___ is a fraction in which the numerator is larger than the denominator.

5. The top number of a fraction is the ___.

More Practice *Show your work on a separate sheet of paper.*

What fraction of each picture is shaded?

6.   7.    8. 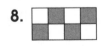   9.

Write each mixed number as an improper fraction.

10. $2\frac{3}{4}$ 11. $3\frac{1}{2}$ 12. $1\frac{7}{8}$ 13. $5\frac{3}{10}$

Write each improper fraction as a whole number or a mixed number.

14. $\frac{10}{3}$ 15. $\frac{12}{4}$ 16. $\frac{5}{2}$ 17. $\frac{9}{5}$

Write each fraction in lowest terms.

18. $\frac{10}{20}$ 19. $\frac{6}{9}$ 20. $\frac{12}{15}$ 21. $\frac{20}{24}$

Tell which fraction is larger.

22. $\frac{1}{2}$ or $\frac{2}{3}$ 23. $\frac{3}{4}$ or $\frac{2}{3}$ 24. $\frac{4}{5}$ or $\frac{2}{3}$ 25. $\frac{4}{5}$ or $\frac{4}{7}$

Add or subtract. Write the answer in lowest terms.

26. $\frac{2}{9} + \frac{5}{9}$ 27. $\frac{7}{10} - \frac{3}{10}$ 28. $\frac{5}{6} + \frac{5}{6}$ 29. $1 - \frac{1}{3}$

30. $\frac{3}{4} + \frac{3}{5}$ 31. $\frac{5}{9} - \frac{1}{2}$ 32. $\frac{5}{12} + \frac{3}{4}$ 33. $\frac{1}{3} - \frac{2}{9}$

34. $4\frac{3}{7} + 6\frac{2}{7}$ 35. $3 - \frac{1}{10}$ 36. $8\frac{1}{4} + 6\frac{2}{3}$ 37. $4\frac{1}{5} - 3\frac{2}{3}$

38. $6 + \frac{2}{3}$ 39. $2\frac{3}{10} - \frac{5}{12}$ 40. $3\frac{1}{2} + 2\frac{3}{4}$ 41. $5\frac{2}{3} - 3\frac{1}{2}$

42. $1\frac{5}{6} + \frac{1}{4}$ 43. $3\frac{1}{2} - 1\frac{4}{5}$ 44. $\frac{7}{9} + 3\frac{1}{2}$ 45. $6\frac{1}{4} - \frac{3}{8}$

Problems You Can Solve

Use the chocolate chip cookie recipe from the beginning of this chapter to help you answer Problems 46–51.

46. How many cups of butter, flour, white sugar, brown sugar, nuts, and chocolate chips are used in the recipe all together?

47. If you decided to take the nuts out of the recipe, how many cups of ingredients would you be left with (not counting eggs, baking soda, and vanilla)?

48. How much flour is needed to make two batches of cookies? How much brown sugar? White sugar?

49. How much more brown sugar than white sugar is used in the recipe?

50. Which is there more of in the recipe: flour or chocolate chips? Explain.

51. If the chocolate chips come in a 3-cup bag, how much will be left over?

Chocolate Chip Cookies
$\frac{1}{2}$ cup butter
2 eggs
$2\frac{1}{3}$ cups flour
$\frac{3}{4}$ cup brown sugar
$\frac{1}{2}$ cup white sugar
1 teaspoon baking soda
1 teaspoon vanilla extract
$\frac{2}{3}$ cup chopped nuts
$2\frac{1}{4}$ cups chocolate chips

Write each mixed number as an improper fraction.

1. $1\frac{1}{2}$
2. $3\frac{2}{3}$
3. $2\frac{1}{5}$
4. $1\frac{3}{4}$

Write each improper fraction as a whole number or a mixed number.

5. $\frac{9}{4}$
6. $\frac{10}{5}$
7. $\frac{13}{6}$
8. $\frac{9}{2}$

Write each fraction in lowest terms.

9. $\frac{12}{18}$
10. $\frac{12}{24}$
11. $\frac{9}{15}$
12. $\frac{16}{48}$

Tell which fraction is larger.

13. $\frac{3}{5}$ or $\frac{3}{4}$
14. $\frac{1}{3}$ or $\frac{1}{5}$
15. $\frac{5}{6}$ or $\frac{2}{3}$
16. $\frac{7}{9}$ or $\frac{5}{6}$

Add or subtract. Write the answer in lowest terms.

17. $\frac{6}{7} - \frac{2}{7}$
18. $\frac{2}{5} + \frac{3}{5}$
19. $\frac{3}{8} + \frac{5}{6}$
20. $1 - \frac{1}{2}$

21. $\frac{2}{3} - \frac{4}{9}$
22. $3\frac{1}{5} - 2\frac{1}{3}$
23. $2\frac{1}{2} - 1\frac{2}{3}$
24. $1\frac{1}{6} + 1\frac{2}{3}$

25. $4\frac{1}{4} + 2\frac{1}{2}$
26. $5\frac{1}{2} - \frac{3}{4}$
27. $7\frac{1}{2} + 2\frac{1}{2}$
28. $8\frac{3}{4} - 2\frac{1}{6}$

29. $12 + \frac{3}{7}$
30. $6\frac{1}{5} + 3\frac{1}{2}$
31. $10 - \frac{3}{8}$
32. $\frac{4}{5} + 2\frac{2}{3}$

Solve the problems.

33. Ana made 8 out of 12 free throws. Write the number of free throws she made as a fraction in lowest terms.

34. What fraction of a dollar is 5 cents?

35. Barry's parents each offered to loan him part of the cost of a new bicycle. His father offered to pay $\frac{2}{3}$ of the cost. His mother offered to pay $\frac{2}{5}$. Who offered to pay more?

36. Zack bought $\frac{1}{2}$ dozen chocolate chip cookies and $\frac{7}{12}$ dozen peanut butter cookies. How many dozen cookies did he buy?

37. Sherry spent $3\frac{3}{4}$ hours at the mall. She spent $\frac{5}{6}$ hour eating lunch in the mall's food court. How much time did Sherry spend shopping?

38. Robert has a board 9 feet long. He wants to cut off 3 pieces that are $2\frac{4}{5}$ feet, $2\frac{3}{4}$ feet, and $3\frac{1}{2}$ feet. How much too short is the board?

Chapter 4
Multiplying and Dividing Fractions and Mixed Numbers

In this chapter, you will learn

- To multiply fractions
- To simplify fractions before multiplying
- To multiply mixed numbers
- To find the reciprocal of a number
- To divide fractions
- To divide mixed numbers
- To write fractions as decimals
- To compare decimals and fractions

The Boys and Girls Club is holding a flea market and craft show to raise money. They are setting up $10\frac{1}{2}$-foot-long tables end-to-end down the center of a tent that is 168 feet long. Mrs. Rodriguez, who is helping to organize the flea market, is keeping track of the table requests.

How many tables can fit end-to-end down the center of the tent? How many feet of table space does the Carrera family want? How many feet does the Rodriguez family want? If the Rodriguez family divides their table space into 3 equal sections, how long will each section be?

When you are with family and friends you will find that you sometimes need to use fractions. In this chapter, you will learn how to find the answers to these and other questions involving multiplying and dividing fractions and mixed numbers.

Family	Tables Requested
Carrera	$\frac{3}{4}$
Thompson	$1\frac{1}{2}$
Rodriguez	$2\frac{1}{4}$
Matthews	2

➤ 4.1 Multiplying Fractions

In This Lesson, You Will Learn

To multiply fractions

To simplify fractions before multiplying

Words to Learn

Simplify to write a problem or fraction in lowest terms by dividing by common factors of the numerator and denominator

---

The Simmons family mailed invitations for a family reunion. Of all the family members invited, $\frac{3}{4}$ respond. Of these responses, $\frac{1}{2}$ say they will attend the reunion. What fraction of the family members who responded will attend?

New Idea

To find the number of people who will attend the reunion, you need to find $\frac{1}{2}$ of $\frac{3}{4}$. You have to multiply $\frac{1}{2} \times \frac{3}{4}$. Look at the parts where the shadings for $\frac{1}{2}$ and $\frac{3}{4}$ overlap. 3 of 8 equal parts are shaded. $\frac{3}{8}$ is shaded.

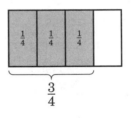 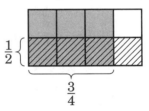

You can also use multiplication to find the product. To multiply fractions, multiply the numerators and multiply the denominators. Write in lowest terms.

$$\frac{1}{2} \times \frac{3}{4} = \frac{1 \times 3}{2 \times 4} = \frac{3}{8}$$

The product of $\frac{1}{2}$ and $\frac{3}{4}$ is $\frac{3}{8}$.

Example: Find $\frac{2}{3}$ of $\frac{5}{8}$.

Step 1: Multiply the fractions by multiplying the numerators, then multiplying the denominators.

$$\frac{2}{3} \times \frac{5}{8} = \frac{2 \times 5}{3 \times 8} = \frac{10}{24}$$

Step 2: Write the product in lowest terms. The greatest common factor of 10 and 24 is 2. Divide 10 and 24 by 2.

$$\frac{10}{24} = \frac{10 \div 2}{24 \div 2} = \frac{5}{12}$$

$\frac{2}{3}$ of $\frac{5}{8}$ is $\frac{5}{12}$.

Sometimes you will need to multiply whole numbers and fractions. One way to multiply whole numbers by fractions is to remember that a fraction counts parts of a whole.

$\frac{3}{4}$ of 20 is 15.

To find $\frac{3}{4}$ of 20, think of $\frac{3}{4}$ as 3 of 4 equal parts. Divide 20 into 4 equal parts and count the amount in 3 of the parts.

You can also multiply a whole number and a fraction. Change the whole number to a fraction. Then multiply the numerators and denominators. Write the fraction in lowest terms.

Example: Find $\frac{2}{5}$ of 42.

Step 1: Write 42 as a fraction.

$$\frac{2}{5} \times 42 = \frac{2}{5} \times \frac{42}{1}$$

Step 2: Multiply the numerators. Multiply the denominators.

$$\frac{2 \times 42}{5 \times 1} = \frac{84}{5}$$

Step 3: Write the improper fraction as a mixed number. Divide 84 by 5.

$$\frac{84}{5} = 16\frac{4}{5}$$

$\frac{2}{5}$ of 42 is $16\frac{4}{5}$.

Focus on the Idea

To multiply fractions, multiply the numerators. Then multiply the denominators. Write the fraction in lowest terms.

Practice *Show your work on a separate sheet of paper.*

Multiply. Write the answer in lowest terms.

1. $\frac{1}{5} \times \frac{1}{3}$ 2. $\frac{2}{6} \times \frac{3}{4}$ 3. $\frac{3}{9} \times \frac{1}{2}$ 4. $\frac{4}{5} \times 30$

5. $\frac{5}{9} \times \frac{4}{5}$ 6. $10 \times \frac{5}{8}$ 7. $\frac{2}{10} \times \frac{2}{3}$ 8. $\frac{1}{3} \times \frac{4}{7}$

9. $\frac{1}{2} \times \frac{1}{2}$ 10. $4 \times \frac{1}{5}$ 11. $\frac{1}{6} \times \frac{4}{5}$ 12. $\frac{3}{4} \times 12$

Extend the Idea

Sometimes you can **simplify** a problem before multiplying. To simplify, look for a common factor of the numerator and denominator; divide that numerator and denominator by the common factor. You may be able to do this more than once.

Example 1: Multiply $\frac{3}{8} \times \frac{4}{5}$.

Step 1: Find common factors in the numerator and denominator. There are no common factors between 3 and 8, 3 and 5, or 4 and 5.
4 is the greatest common factor of 4 and 8. Divide 4 and 8 by 4.
$4 \div 4 = 1$ and $8 \div 4 = 2$

$$\frac{3 \times 4}{8 \times 5}$$

$$\frac{3 \times \cancel{4}^{1}}{{}_{2}\cancel{8} \times 5}$$

Step 2: Multiply the numerators. Multiply the denominators.

$$\frac{3 \times 1}{2 \times 5} = \frac{3}{10}$$

The product of $\frac{3}{8}$ and $\frac{4}{5}$ is $\frac{3}{10}$.

Example 2: Multiply $\frac{5}{12} \times \frac{8}{15}$.

Step 1: Find common factors in the numerators and the denominators.

$$\frac{5}{12} \times \frac{8}{15}$$

5 is the greatest common factor of 5 and 15. Divide 5 and 15 by 5.
$5 \div 5 = 1$ and $15 \div 5 = 3$

$$\frac{{}^{1}\cancel{5} \times 8}{12 \times \cancel{15}_{3}}$$

4 is the greatest common factor of 8 and 12. Divide 8 and 12 by 4.
$8 \div 4 = 2$ and $12 \div 4 = 3$

$$\frac{{}^{1}\cancel{5} \times \cancel{8}^{2}}{{}_{3}\cancel{12} \times \cancel{15}_{3}}$$

Step 2: Multiply the numerators. Multiply the denominators.

$$\frac{1 \times 2}{3 \times 3} = \frac{2}{9}$$

The product of $\frac{5}{12}$ and $\frac{8}{15}$ is $\frac{2}{9}$.

Example 3: Multiply $\frac{7}{8} \times \frac{8}{7}$.

Step 1: Find common factors in the numerators and the denominators.
7 is the greatest common factor of 7 and 7. 8 is the greatest common factor of 8 and 8.

$$\frac{7 \times 8}{8 \times 7} = \frac{{}^{1}\cancel{7} \times \cancel{8}^{1}}{{}_{1}\cancel{8} \times \cancel{7}_{1}}$$

Step 2: Multiply the numerators. Multiply the denominators.

$$\frac{1 \times 1}{1 \times 1} = \frac{1}{1} = 1$$

The product of $\frac{7}{8}$ and $\frac{8}{7}$ is 1.

✓ Check the Math

John is finding the product of $\frac{2}{3}$ and $\frac{4}{5}$.

$$\frac{2}{3} \times \frac{4}{5} = \frac{{}^1\cancel{2} \times \cancel{4}^2}{3 \times 5} = \frac{1 \times 2}{3 \times 5} = \frac{2}{15}$$

Is he correct? Why or why not?

Practice *Show your work on a separate sheet of paper.*
Multiply. Try to simplify before you multiply.

13. $\frac{2}{4} \times \frac{1}{6}$ 14. $\frac{1}{2} \times 12$ 15. $\frac{2}{3} \times \frac{3}{2}$ 16. $\frac{4}{5} \times \frac{5}{8}$

17. $\frac{2}{9} \times \frac{3}{5}$ 18. $\frac{1}{4} \times 20$ 19. $\frac{5}{6} \times \frac{9}{10}$ 20. $\frac{5}{4} \times \frac{4}{5}$

21. $13 \times \frac{9}{26}$ 22. $\frac{5}{8} \times \frac{2}{15}$ 23. $15 \times \frac{3}{10}$ 24. $\frac{8}{9} \times \frac{2}{12}$

25. $\frac{3}{8} \times \frac{1}{3}$ 26. $\frac{1}{6} \times 6$ 27. $\frac{9}{16} \times \frac{2}{3}$ 28. $\frac{4}{5} \times \frac{1}{2}$

Apply the Idea

29. There are 20 high school students at the reunion. $\frac{2}{5}$ of them wear braces. How many wear braces?

30. There was $\frac{3}{8}$ of a cake left over. Aunt Harriet took $\frac{1}{4}$ of what was left. How much did she take?

31. 18 people were surveyed. $\frac{2}{3}$ of them speak a foreign language. How many speak a foreign language?

✎ Write About It

32. Why is it helpful to divide by common factors before multiplying fractions?

⬇ 4.2 Multiplying Mixed Numbers

In This Lesson, You Will Learn
To multiply mixed numbers

Words to Learn
Double to multiply by 2

Mixed number a number written with a whole number and a fraction

---

Joel is baking cookies for a picnic. The recipe calls for $1\frac{1}{3}$ cups of flour. To make enough cookies for everyone at the picnic, Joel has to double the recipe. How much flour will he need?

New Idea

To **double** the recipe, Joel needs two times the amount of flour. He needs $1\frac{1}{3}$ cups and then another $1\frac{1}{3}$ cups.

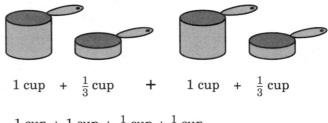

1 cup + $\frac{1}{3}$ cup + 1 cup + $\frac{1}{3}$ cup

You also can double $1\frac{1}{3}$ by multiplying the **mixed number** by 2. First change the mixed number to an improper fraction.

1 cup + 1 cup + $\frac{1}{3}$ cup + $\frac{1}{3}$ cup

$2\frac{2}{3}$ cups

$$1\frac{1}{3} \times 2 = \frac{4}{3} \times 2$$

Then multiply the numerators and denominators. Change the improper fraction to a mixed number.

$$\frac{4}{3} \times \frac{2}{1} = \frac{4 \times 2}{3 \times 1} = \frac{8}{3} = 2\frac{2}{3}$$

The product of $1\frac{1}{3}$ and 2 is $2\frac{2}{3}$.

Example: Multiply $3\frac{1}{4} \times 2\frac{2}{5}$.

Step 1: Write each mixed number as an improper fraction.

$$\frac{13}{4} \times \frac{12}{5}$$

Step 2: Simplify, if possible, then multiply the numerators and the denominators.

$$\frac{13 \times \cancel{12}^{3}}{\cancel{4}_{1} \times 5} = \frac{13 \times 3}{1 \times 5} = \frac{39}{5}$$

Step 3: Write the improper fraction as a mixed number.

The product of $3\frac{1}{4}$ and $2\frac{2}{5}$ is $7\frac{4}{5}$.

$$\frac{39}{5} = 7\frac{4}{5}$$

Focus on the Idea

To multiply mixed numbers, change each mixed number to an improper fraction. Simplify if possible. Then multiply the numerators and multiply the denominators. If the product is an improper fraction, write it as a mixed number.

Practice *Show your work on a separate sheet of paper.*

Multiply. Write the answer in lowest terms.

1. $1\frac{1}{3} \times 1\frac{1}{5}$

2. $4\frac{1}{2} \times 3\frac{1}{6}$

3. $2\frac{2}{3} \times 2\frac{2}{3}$

4. $\frac{3}{5} \times 1\frac{3}{4}$

5. $2\frac{2}{7} \times 3\frac{1}{6}$

6. $5\frac{1}{3} \times 3\frac{3}{8}$

7. $3\frac{1}{2} \times \frac{2}{7}$

8. $2\frac{3}{4} \times 1\frac{1}{4}$

9. $\frac{1}{2} \times 3\frac{2}{3}$

10. $4 \times 4\frac{1}{4}$

11. $1\frac{4}{9} \times \frac{1}{3}$

12. $5\frac{1}{2} \times 2\frac{3}{4}$

Apply the Idea

Joel bakes four kinds of cookies. Multiply to find how many dozen of each cookie he bakes in Problems 13–16.

Cookie	Number of Recipes Made	Dozens from Each Recipe
13. Chocolate	5	$4\frac{1}{2}$
14. Lemon	2	$5\frac{5}{12}$
15. Sugar	2	$2\frac{3}{4}$
16. Peanut Butter	4	$3\frac{1}{3}$

17. Joel has a table $5\frac{3}{4}$ feet long. He only needs a table $\frac{2}{3}$ of that length. What length table does he need?

Write About It

18. It takes Joel 55 minutes of preparation time and 15 minutes of baking time to make a batch of cookies. Explain how you could use multiplication to find the number of hours it would take him to make 3 batches of cookies. (**Hint:** Express the minutes as a fraction of an hour. Remember that an hour has 60 minutes.)

➤ 4.3 Dividing Fractions

In This Lesson, You Will learn

To find the reciprocal of a number

To divide fractions

Words to Learn

Reciprocal numbers two numbers that when multiplied have 1 as their product

---

Cara is making a banner for the pep rally that is $\frac{3}{4}$ yard long. How many letters can she put on it if each letter takes up $\frac{1}{8}$ yard?

New Idea

Cara needs to find out how many $\frac{1}{8}$ yards fit into $\frac{3}{4}$ yard. She has to divide $\frac{3}{4}$ by $\frac{1}{8}$.

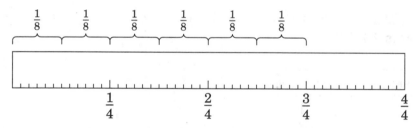

The picture shows that there are six $\frac{1}{8}$ yards in $\frac{3}{4}$ of a yard, or $\frac{3}{4}$ divided by $\frac{1}{8}$ is 6.

$$\frac{3}{4} \div \frac{1}{8} = 6$$

Dividing by $\frac{1}{8}$ is the same as multiplying by 8.

$$\frac{3}{\underset{1}{\cancel{4}}} \times \frac{\cancel{8}^2}{1} = \frac{6}{1} = 6$$

$\frac{1}{8}$ and 8 are called **reciprocal numbers**. The product of a number and its reciprocal is always 1. To find the reciprocal of a fraction, switch the numerator and the denominator.

To divide fractions, multiply the dividend by the reciprocal of the divisor. The dividend, divisor, and quotient are the parts of a division problem.

$$\frac{3}{4} \div \frac{1}{8} = 6$$
$$\downarrow \quad \downarrow \quad \downarrow$$
dividend   divisor   quotient

Example: Divide $\frac{2}{3}$ by $\frac{3}{4}$.

Step 1: Find the reciprocal of the divisor.

The reciprocal of $\frac{3}{4}$ is $\frac{4}{3}$.

Step 2: Multiply the dividend by the reciprocal of the divisor.

$\frac{2}{3} \times \frac{4}{3}$

Step 3: Multiply the numerators. Multiply the denominators.

$\frac{2}{3} \times \frac{4}{3} = \frac{2 \times 4}{3 \times 3} = \frac{8}{9}$

$\frac{2}{3} \div \frac{3}{4} = \frac{8}{9}$

Focus on the Idea

To divide fractions, find the reciprocal of the divisor. Then multiply the dividend by the reciprocal of the divisor. Rename improper fractions and write the answer in lowest terms.

Practice *Show your work on a separate sheet of paper.*

Divide. Write the answer in lowest terms.

1. $\frac{1}{3} \div \frac{1}{6}$

2. $\frac{1}{4} \div \frac{1}{2}$

3. $\frac{3}{5} \div \frac{1}{5}$

4. $\frac{3}{7} \div \frac{3}{4}$

5. $6 \div \frac{3}{8}$

6. $\frac{4}{5} \div \frac{2}{3}$

7. $\frac{1}{2} \div 5$

8. $\frac{7}{9} \div \frac{2}{3}$

9. $\frac{5}{6} \div \frac{5}{6}$

10. $\frac{2}{13} \div \frac{1}{26}$

11. $\frac{4}{5} \div 8$

12. $5 \div \frac{3}{5}$

13. $1 \div \frac{2}{3}$

14. $\frac{4}{9} \div 4$

15. $\frac{1}{4} \div \frac{2}{3}$

16. $\frac{1}{6} \div \frac{1}{3}$

Apply the Idea

17. Cara's banner is $\frac{2}{3}$ yard high. The letters are $\frac{1}{6}$ yard high. How many rows of letters can she fit on the banner?

18. Megan has 4 yards of fabric. How many banners can she make if each banner is $\frac{7}{8}$ yard wide?

Write About It

19. Explain how you would find the reciprocal of a mixed number such as $1\frac{1}{2}$.

4.4 Dividing Mixed Numbers

In This Lesson, You Will Learn
To divide mixed numbers

Jason's baby sister sleeps for $3\frac{1}{2}$ hours. If Jason's mother asks him to check on her every $\frac{1}{2}$ hour, how many times does he check?

New Idea

To find how many times Jason checks on his sister in $3\frac{1}{2}$ hours, you need to find the number of $\frac{1}{2}$ hours in $3\frac{1}{2}$.

 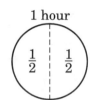 

From the picture, you can see that there are seven $\frac{1}{2}$-hours in $3\frac{1}{2}$ hours, so Jason checks on his sister 7 times. You can also find the number of $\frac{1}{2}$ hours by dividing $3\frac{1}{2}$ by $\frac{1}{2}$. To divide mixed numbers, begin by writing any whole or mixed numbers as improper fractions.

$$3\frac{1}{2} \div \frac{1}{2} = \frac{7}{2} \div \frac{1}{2}$$

To divide the fractions, multiply the dividend by the reciprocal of the divisor. Simplify, if possible. Then multiply the numerators and multiply the denominators.

$$\frac{7}{2} \times \frac{2}{1} = \frac{7 \times \cancel{2}^{1}}{{}_{1}\cancel{2} \times 1} = \frac{7}{1} = 7$$

The quotient of $3\frac{1}{2} \div \frac{1}{2}$ is 7.

When you divide fractions, the quotient is not always a whole number; sometimes it is a mixed number. The fractional remainder tells you what portion of the divisor is left over.

Example: Find the number of $1\frac{3}{4}$-foot pieces you can cut from a board that is 5 feet long. Divide $5 \div 1\frac{3}{4}$.

Step 1: Write the whole number and mixed number as improper fractions. $\qquad 5 \div 1\frac{3}{4} = \frac{5}{1} \div \frac{7}{4}$

Step 2:	Multiply the dividend by the reciprocal of the divisor.		$\frac{5}{1} \times \frac{4}{7}$
Step 3:	Simplify, if possible. Multiply the numerators. Multiply the denominators.		$\frac{5}{1} \times \frac{4}{7} = \frac{5 \times 4}{1 \times 7} = \frac{20}{7}$
Step 4:	Write the improper fraction as a mixed number.		$\frac{20}{7} = 2\frac{6}{7}$

The quotient of $5 \div 1\frac{3}{4}$ is $2\frac{6}{7}$. You can cut 2 pieces, $1\frac{3}{4}$ feet in length, from a 5-foot board. $\frac{6}{7}$ of a $1\frac{3}{4}$-foot piece is left over.

Focus on the Idea

To divide mixed numbers, change mixed numbers to improper fractions. Multiply the dividend by the reciprocal of the divisor. Write the quotient as a mixed number in lowest terms.

Practice *Show your work on a separate sheet of paper.*

Divide. Write the answer in lowest terms.

1. $2\frac{1}{2} \div 1\frac{1}{3}$ 2. $4\frac{1}{8} \div 1\frac{1}{4}$ 3. $5\frac{3}{7} \div 3\frac{1}{2}$ 4. $10 \div 1\frac{2}{3}$

5. $3\frac{3}{4} \div 1\frac{2}{7}$ 6. $2\frac{1}{7} \div 4$ 7. $5\frac{1}{4} \div 1\frac{5}{7}$ 8. $6\frac{3}{4} \div 3\frac{3}{8}$

9. $4\frac{1}{2} \div 1\frac{1}{4}$ 10. $3\frac{3}{5} \div 1\frac{1}{8}$ 11. $8\frac{1}{7} \div 2\frac{5}{7}$ 12. $7 \div 3\frac{1}{3}$

Apply the Idea

Jason makes planters for his mother. He has boards in lengths of 8 feet. He has a list of the lengths of the pieces he needs to cut from the 8-foot boards. Divide to find the number of pieces of each length he can cut from an 8-foot board.

13. $2\frac{1}{3}$ feet

14. $1\frac{3}{8}$ feet

15. $1\frac{1}{2}$ feet

16. $1\frac{3}{4}$ feet

Write About It

17. Suppose you spend $7\frac{1}{2}$ hours painting. You finish a gallon of paint every $2\frac{1}{4}$ hours. Explain how you could use division to find the number of gallons used.

4.5 Writing Fractions as Decimals and Decimals as Fractions

In This Lesson, You Will Learn

To write fractions as decimals

To compare decimals and fractions

Theo bikes from school to the library. His bike's odometer, which measures the distance traveled, reads .75 miles. Sherrie says the distance is $\frac{3}{4}$ mile. How can they compare the two numbers to see whether they agree?

New Idea

To compare the numbers, Theo and Sherrie must write both numbers as decimals or both numbers as fractions. Fractions and decimals both name parts of wholes. So, you can change any fraction to a decimal.

One way to change a fraction to a decimal is to find an equivalent fraction with a denominator of 10, 100, or 1,000. Then write the equivalent fraction as a decimal.

Step 1: Try to find an equivalent fraction with a denominator of 10.

$$\frac{3}{4} = \frac{?}{10}$$

4 does not divide evenly into 10, so next try finding a denominator of 100.

$$\frac{3}{4} = \frac{?}{100}$$

$$100 \div 4 = 25$$
$$3 \times 25 = 75$$

Step 2: Write 75 hundredths as a decimal. $\frac{3}{4}$ is the same as .75.

$$\frac{3}{4} = \frac{75}{100} = .75$$

Remember that one decimal place represents tenths, two decimal places represent hundredths, three decimal places represent thousandths, and so on.

If the denominator of the fraction does not divide evenly into 10, 100, or 1000, you can use division to change a fraction to a decimal. Divide the numerator by the denominator. Add a decimal point and zeros to the dividend until there is no remainder or until you have 4 decimal places. Round to 3 decimal places.

Example: Write $\frac{3}{8}$ as a decimal.

Divide 3 by 8.

Write a decimal point in the numerator, and continue adding zeros and dividing until there is no remainder or you have 4 decimal places.

$\frac{3}{8} = .375$

$$\begin{array}{r} .375 \\ 8\overline{)3.000} \\ -24 \\ \hline 60 \\ -56 \\ \hline 40 \\ -40 \\ \hline 0 \end{array}$$

 When you use a calculator to divide, your result may have many decimal places. Round to 3 decimal places.

To write $\frac{5}{9}$ as a decimal: 5 $\boxed{\div}$ 9 $\boxed{=}$ .5555555

Round to the nearest thousandth. → .556

$\frac{5}{9}$ is about .556.

Focus on the Idea

To write a fraction as a decimal, find an equivalent fraction with a numerator of 10, 100, or 1,000 and write it as a decimal, or divide the numerator by the denominator.

Practice *Show your work on a separate sheet of paper.*

Write each fraction as a decimal.

1. $\frac{1}{2}$ 2. $\frac{1}{4}$ 3. $\frac{1}{5}$ 4. $\frac{2}{5}$ 5. $\frac{3}{5}$ 6. $\frac{1}{8}$ 7. $\frac{5}{8}$ 8. $\frac{7}{8}$

 Write each fraction as a decimal.

9. $\frac{1}{3}$ 10. $\frac{2}{7}$ 11. $\frac{4}{9}$ 12. $\frac{5}{12}$

Change the fraction to a decimal. Tell which number is larger.

13. $\frac{1}{2}$ .48   14. $\frac{3}{8}$ .4   15. $\frac{2}{3}$ .6   16. $\frac{3}{4}$ .8

Apply the Idea

17. The coach of Theo's bike team told him to ride at least $2\frac{1}{2}$ miles every day. According to his odometer, Theo rode a total of 6.9 miles in 3 days. Did he ride as many miles as his coach told him to?

Write About It

18. Why do you think some things are measured in fractions while others are measured in decimals?

Chapter 4 Review

In this chapter, you have learned
- To multiply fractions
- To simplify fractions before multiplying
- To multiply mixed numbers
- To find the reciprocal of a number
- To divide fractions
- To divide mixed numbers
- To write fractions as decimals
- To compare decimals and fractions

Words You Know

From the lists of Words to Learn, choose the word or phrase that best completes each statement.

1. ___ are numbers that when multiplied have 1 as their product.

2. When you ___ fractions before multiplying, your answer will be in lowest terms.

3. A number written with a whole number and a fraction is called a ___.

More Practice *Show your work on a separate sheet of paper.*

Multiply. Write the answer in lowest terms.

4. $\frac{1}{2} \times \frac{2}{3}$

5. $\frac{3}{8} \times \frac{1}{6}$

6. $\frac{4}{9} \times \frac{7}{8}$

7. $\frac{5}{9} \times \frac{9}{5}$

8. $\frac{9}{10} \times \frac{5}{18}$

9. $\frac{1}{2} \times \frac{1}{2}$

10. $2\frac{1}{4} \times 1\frac{5}{6}$

11. $5\frac{1}{5} \times 2\frac{1}{2}$

12. $6 \times 1\frac{1}{3}$

13. $\frac{3}{5} \times 2$

14. $1\frac{1}{3} \times \frac{1}{6}$

15. $3 \times 1\frac{2}{9}$

16. $2\frac{1}{2} \times 2\frac{1}{2}$

17. $\frac{1}{4} \times 2\frac{4}{5}$

18. $3\frac{5}{8} \times 3\frac{1}{4}$

19. $1\frac{5}{16} \times \frac{4}{7}$

Find the reciprocal of each number.

20. $\frac{2}{3}$

21. $\frac{1}{6}$

22. 5

23. $2\frac{3}{4}$

Divide. Write the answer in lowest terms.

24. $\frac{1}{4} \div \frac{1}{8}$

25. $\frac{2}{3} \div \frac{2}{3}$

26. $\frac{5}{9} \div \frac{1}{3}$

27. $\frac{3}{4} \div 3$

28. $\frac{2}{5} \div \frac{5}{2}$

29. $5 \div \frac{1}{7}$

30. $\frac{4}{5} \div 4$

31. $2\frac{1}{2} \div 5$

32. $8 \div \frac{1}{3}$ **33.** $3\frac{3}{8} \div 2\frac{1}{4}$ **34.** $1\frac{3}{4} \div 2\frac{4}{7}$ **35.** $2\frac{2}{9} \div \frac{1}{9}$

36. $6\frac{1}{4} \div 2\frac{1}{2}$ **37.** $\frac{1}{2} \div 6$ **38.** $5 \div \frac{1}{5}$ **39.** $3\frac{1}{3} \div \frac{5}{9}$

Write each fraction as a decimal.

40. $\frac{2}{5}$ **41.** $\frac{3}{4}$ **42.** $\frac{3}{8}$ **43.** $\frac{4}{10}$ **44.** $\frac{1}{3}$

45. $\frac{2}{3}$ **46.** $\frac{5}{8}$ **47.** $\frac{25}{50}$ **48.** $\frac{2}{9}$ **49.** $\frac{4}{9}$

Order the numbers from least to greatest.

50. $.4, \frac{2}{3}, \frac{1}{2}$ **51.** $.82, \frac{3}{4}, \frac{5}{6}$ **52.** $\frac{1}{9}, .12, .11$ **53.** $\frac{3}{8}, .38, .4$

Problems You Can Solve

Use this chart of table requests for the Boys and Girls Club flea market and crafts show to answer Problems 54–60. Each table is $10\frac{1}{2}$ feet long.

Family	Tables Requested
Carrera	$\frac{3}{4}$
Thompson	$1\frac{1}{2}$
Rodriguez	$2\frac{1}{4}$
Matthews	2

54. The flea market and craft show is being held in a tent that measures 168 feet long. How many $10\frac{1}{2}$-foot tables can fit end-to-end down the center of the tent?

55. How many feet of table space does the Carrera family want?

56. If the Thompsons can fit 12 handcrafted birdhouses on a table, how many can they display in the space they have requested?

57. How many feet of table space does the Rodriguez family want?

58. If the Rodriguez family divides their table space into 3 equal sections, how long will each section be?

59. If Mrs. Rodriguez spent 2.6 hours setting up tables one morning and Mrs. Matthews spent $\frac{1}{2}$ hour and another $2\frac{1}{4}$ hours the morning before, who spent more time setting up?

60. The flea market will last 8 hours. How many $2\frac{1}{2}$-hour shifts are there in 8 hours?

Chapter 4 Practice Test

Multiply. Write the answer in lowest terms.

1. $\frac{3}{5} \times \frac{1}{2}$

2. $\frac{3}{4} \times \frac{2}{9}$

3. $\frac{1}{8} \times \frac{4}{5}$

4. $\frac{2}{5} \times \frac{5}{2}$

5. $\frac{3}{4} \times 4$

6. $2\frac{3}{8} \times 4\frac{2}{3}$

7. $2\frac{3}{4} \times 5\frac{1}{2}$

8. $3\frac{1}{6} \times 4\frac{1}{3}$

9. $3\frac{5}{7} \times 2\frac{9}{13}$

Divide. Write the answer in lowest terms.

10. $\frac{1}{2} \div \frac{1}{5}$

11. $\frac{4}{7} \div \frac{8}{14}$

12. $\frac{6}{7} \div 4$

13. $1\frac{5}{6} \div \frac{1}{4}$

14. $6 \div 1\frac{1}{3}$

15. $3\frac{3}{4} \div 2\frac{3}{8}$

16. $2\frac{2}{5} \div 5\frac{1}{2}$

17. $1\frac{2}{7} \div 2\frac{2}{7}$

18. $5\frac{1}{2} \div 3$

Write each fraction as a decimal.

19. $\frac{3}{5}$

20. $\frac{3}{6}$

21. $\frac{3}{4}$

22. $\frac{2}{3}$

Write the numbers in order from least to greatest.

23. $\frac{2}{5}, .41, \frac{7}{15}$

24. $.5, \frac{3}{8}, \frac{4}{7}$

25. $.223, \frac{2}{9}, .2$

26. $.34, \frac{4}{9}, .43$

Solve the problems.

27. Rachel is making cookies. The recipe calls for $2\frac{2}{3}$ cups of sugar. If she makes the recipe $3\frac{1}{4}$ times, how much sugar does she need?

28. How many cookies can Rachel get from the recipe if it makes $5\frac{1}{4}$ dozen cookies?

29. Of the cookies Rachel makes, $\frac{2}{3}$ are chocolate. $\frac{1}{2}$ of these have nuts. What fraction of all the cookies have nuts?

30. Ben needs to cut a 10-foot board into lengths that are $2\frac{1}{2}$ feet long. How many pieces can he cut from the board?

31. Ben has a board that is $5\frac{7}{8}$ feet long.
    a. How many $\frac{3}{4}$-foot pieces can he cut?
    b. How much board will be left over?

32. Sal mows his neighbor's yard. He earns $15 for $2\frac{1}{5}$ hours of work. How much does he earn per hour?

33. Sal also cleans the gutters of his neighbor's house. He earns $28 dollars for $3\frac{1}{3}$ hours work. How much does he earn per hour?

Chapter 5
Ratios and Proportions

In this chapter, you will learn

- To understand and write ratios
- To use ratios and proportions
- To find the missing number in a proportion by cross-multiplying and dividing
- To solve proportions involving scale

Aaron is part of the photography team on his school's yearbook committee. He develops film and makes 4-inch wide by 6-inch long prints. Kara, the yearbook's art director, must size these pieces to fit the space available. She can either reduce or enlarge a photo to fit in an available space, as long as the photo's measurements stay in the same proportion. To design the yearbook, Kara uses a computer program that lets her view a whole page by reducing it to scale.

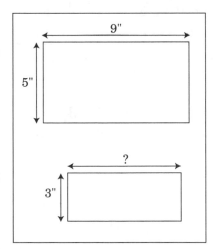

If Aaron gives Kara only 5 of the 24 pictures he takes at an event, what is the ratio of the pictures he submits to the pictures he takes? Can Kara enlarge Aaron's photos to fit a 5-inch by 9-inch space? If Kara has to include 3 photos for every two pages of the yearbook, how many photos will she need for a 180-page yearbook? If a page appears 8 inches wide on Kara's computer screen, how wide will it be in the yearbook?

If you enjoy photography or hobbies that use patterns and measurements, you have probably run across situations where a ratio or proportion could help you find an answer. In this chapter, you will learn how to use ratios and proportion to solve problems like these.

5.1 Understanding and Writing Ratios

In This Lesson, You Will Learn
To understand and write ratios

Words to Learn
Ratio a comparison of two numbers
Equivalent ratios ratios that have the same value

Mercedes is making a patchwork quilt. On the right is a section of the quilt. The ratio of dark squares to white squares is 4 to 5.

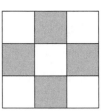

New Idea
A **ratio** compares two numbers. The ratio tells Mercedes that for every 4 dark squares she needs 5 white ones. The order of numbers in a ratio is important. You can write a ratio several ways.

$$4 \text{ to } 5 \qquad 4:5 \qquad \frac{4}{5}$$

Example 1: Find the ratio of white squares to dark squares.

$$\frac{\text{white squares}}{\text{dark squares}} \rightarrow \frac{5}{4}$$

The ratio of white squares to dark squares is 5:4.

Example 2: Find the ratio of white squares to total squares in the quilt section.

$$\frac{\text{white squares}}{\text{total squares}} \rightarrow \frac{5}{9}$$

The ratio of white squares to total squares is 5:9.

You can also find an **equivalent ratio** for 4:5. Equivalent ratios have the same value. To form an equivalent ratio, multiply or divide by the same number.

There are 9 sections in a complete quilt. The ratio of dark squares to white squares stays the same. To form an equivalent ratio that tells you the number of dark squares and white squares in the finished quilt, multiply by 9.

$$\frac{4 \times 9}{5 \times 9} = \frac{36}{45}$$

She needs 36 dark squares and 45 white squares to complete the 9-section quilt.

Focus on the Idea

A ratio compares two quantities.
The ratio 2 to 3 also can be written 2:3 and $\frac{2}{3}$.
To form an equivalent ratio, multiply or divide by the same number.

Practice *Show your work on a separate sheet of paper.*

Write the following ratios.

1. 86 hits every 258 at-bats

2. 60 wins in 75 games

3. 210 CDs to 70 cassettes

4. 3,000 cartoons in 800 pages

5. 15 pillows to 4 quilts

6. 240 miles with 12 gallons

7. 26 miles per 1 gallon

8. 14 calories in 2 grams

Write the ratios described.

9. Sue needs 2 pints of paint for 5 birdhouses.
   a. What is the ratio of pints of paint to birdhouses?
   b. What is the ratio of birdhouses to pints of paint?

10. A state has 15 Olympic champions. 10 are women and 5 are men. What is the ratio of women to men?

Apply the Idea

11. Alexis is knitting a sweater. The pattern calls for 3 balls of navy blue yarn and 1 ball of white yarn.
    a. What is the ratio of white yarn to navy blue yarn?
    b. If she knits 3 sweaters, what is the equivalent ratio?

12. Amanda fills a large planter on her deck using 10 pounds of potting soil and 15 plants.
    a. What is the ratio of pounds of potting soil to the number of plants?
    b. What is the ratio of plants to pounds of potting soil?

13. Amanda decides to make a total of 6 identical planters for her deck. What is the equivalent ratio of pounds of potting soil to plants for the entire project?

Write About It

14. Look at a calendar. Is the ratio of Mondays to days in the month the same for every month? Why or why not?

5.2 Using Ratios and Proportions

In This Lesson, You Will Learn

To use ratios and proportions

To find the missing number in a proportion by
cross-multiplying and dividing

Words to Learn

Proportion a statement that says that two ratios have
the same value

Cross product the product of the numbers diagonally
across from each other in a proportion

Lana is purchasing a sprinkler system for the main lawn of the
Public Garden. She wants to install 3 sprinkler heads for every 200
square feet of lawn. The main lawn measures 1,000 square feet.
How many sprinkler heads should Lana purchase?

New Idea

The ratio of sprinkler heads
to square feet is $\frac{3}{200}$.

Main lawn = 1,000 sq ft

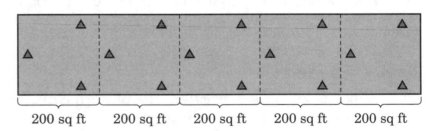

By looking at the picture, you can see that Lana needs 15 sprinkler
heads. The ratio $\frac{3}{200}$ is equivalent to the ratio $\frac{15}{1,000}$. You can write
equivalent ratios as a proportion. A **proportion** is a statement that
says that two ratios have the same value.

$$\frac{\text{sprinklers}}{\text{square feet}} \qquad \frac{3}{200} = \frac{15}{1,000}$$

In a proportion, the cross products are equal. The **cross products**
of a proportion are the products of the numbers diagonally across
from each other.

$$\frac{3}{200} \diagdown\diagup \frac{15}{1,000} \qquad \begin{array}{l} 3 \times 1,000 = 3,000 \\ 15 \times 200 = 3,000 \qquad 3,000 = 3,000 \end{array}$$

If the cross products of two ratios are not equal, they do not form a
true proportion.

Example: Determine whether $\frac{2}{3}$ and $\frac{5}{8}$ form a true proportion.

Find the cross products:

$$\frac{2}{3} \diagdown\!\!\!\!\diagup \frac{5}{8} \qquad \begin{array}{l} 2 \times 8 = 16 \\ 3 \times 5 = 15 \\ \quad 16 \neq 15 \end{array}$$

The cross products are not equal, so the ratios do not form a proportion.

If you know three numbers in a proportion, you can always find the fourth.

Example: 3 sprinklers cost $120. Find the price of 15 sprinklers.

Step 1: Set up a proportion.

$$\frac{\text{sprinklers}}{\text{cost}} = \frac{\text{sprinklers}}{\text{cost}}$$

Step 2: Fill in what you know. Use a question mark for what you are looking for.

$$\frac{3}{120} = \frac{15}{?}$$

Step 3: Find the cross product of the two numbers you know.

$$15 \times 120 = 1{,}800$$

Step 4: Divide the cross product by the third number to find the missing number.

$$1{,}800 \div 3 = 600$$

15 sprinklers cost $600.

$$\frac{3}{120} = \frac{15}{600}$$

Focus on the Idea

A proportion is a statement that says two ratios are equivalent. Solve for a missing number in a proportion by dividing the cross product by the third number.

Practice *Show your work on a separate sheet of paper.*

Find the missing number in each proportion.

1. $\frac{1}{6} = \frac{?}{24}$ 2. $\frac{5}{7} = \frac{35}{?}$ 3. $\frac{?}{12} = \frac{9}{36}$ 4. $\frac{8}{?} = \frac{72}{81}$ 5. $\frac{?}{9} = \frac{2}{3}$

6. $\frac{11}{?} = \frac{88}{40}$ 7. $\frac{2}{5} = \frac{?}{50}$ 8. $\frac{4}{?} = \frac{22}{33}$ 9. $\frac{3}{7} = \frac{?}{28}$ 10. $\frac{5}{8} = \frac{40}{?}$

Apply the Idea

11. Mr. Chang's copier can make 40 copies in 4 minutes. How long will it take to make 2,400 copies? Set up a proportion and solve.

12. Pedro has a photo that is 3 inches wide and 5 inches long. He enlarges it so that the new width is 15 inches. What is the length of the enlarged photo? Set up a proportion and solve.

Write About It

13. Think of a situation in which you could use ratios. Create a ratio problem based on your example.

5.3 Solving Problems with Proportion and Scale

In This Lesson, You Will Learn
To solve proportions involving scale

Words to Learn
Scale drawing a drawing that shows an object or distance in proportion to its real measurements

Scale a ratio that compares the measurements in a drawing or model to the actual measurements

Each season, Pedro calls the New York Yankee box office for a copy of the team's schedule. The schedule includes a scale drawing of the baseball field at Yankee Stadium. The scale of the drawing is 1 centimeter = 30 feet. If the distance between the bases in the drawing is 3 centimeters, how can Pedro figure the actual distance between the bases?

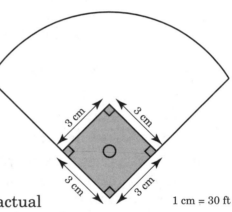

1 cm = 30 ft

New Idea
A **scale drawing** shows an object in proportion to its actual measurements. Pedro can find the distance between the bases by setting up a proportion and then solving it. To set up the proportion, use the scale given in the drawing. The **scale** is the ratio that compares the measurements in the drawing or model to the actual measurements.

Step 1: Write a ratio for the scale.

$$\frac{1 \text{ cm}}{30 \text{ ft}} = \frac{\text{drawing}}{\text{real life}}$$

Step 2: Set up a proportion using what you know. The distance between the bases on the drawing is 3 centimeters.

$$\frac{1 \text{ cm}}{30 \text{ ft}} = \frac{3 \text{ cm}}{? \text{ ft}}$$

Step 3: Cross multiply.

$$3 \times 30 = 90$$

Step 4: Divide by the third number to find the missing number.

$$90 \div 1 = 90$$

A distance of 3 centimeters on the scale drawing equals a distance of 90 feet between the bases.

$$\frac{1 \text{ cm}}{30 \text{ ft}} = \frac{3 \text{ cm}}{90 \text{ ft}}$$

Maps are also usually drawn to scale.

Example: The distance between 2 points on a map measures 1.5 inches. Find the actual distance if the scale on the map says 1 inch = 120 miles.

Step 1: Write a ratio for the scale.

$$\frac{1 \text{ in.}}{120 \text{ mi.}}$$

Step 2: Set up a proportion using what you know.

$$\frac{1 \text{ in.}}{120 \text{ mi.}} = \frac{1.5 \text{ in.}}{? \text{ mi.}}$$

Step 3: Cross multiply.

$$1.5 \times 120 = 180$$

Step 4: Divide by the third number to find the missing number.

$$180 \div 1 = 180$$

A distance of 1.5 inches on the map equals an actual distance of 180 miles.

Focus on the Idea

To solve problems of scale, set up a proportion. Use the scale as one ratio. Use the map or scale drawing measurement for the other ratio. Cross multiply and divide to find the missing number.

ILLINOIS

1 in. = 120 mi.

Practice *Show your work on a separate sheet of paper.*

Use the map measurements below to find the actual distances between cities. Use the map scale: 1 inch = 120 miles.

1. Chicago to Normal: 1 in.

2. Galesburg to Peoria: .375 in.

3. Peoria to Champaign: .625 in.

4. Normal to Peoria: .25 in.

Solve the following problems involving map scale.

5. $\dfrac{1 \text{ in.}}{60 \text{ mi.}} = \dfrac{4 \text{ in.}}{? \text{ mi.}}$ 6. $\dfrac{1 \text{ in.}}{500 \text{ mi.}} = \dfrac{2.5 \text{ in.}}{? \text{ mi.}}$ 7. $\dfrac{1.5 \text{ cm}}{100 \text{ m}} = \dfrac{? \text{ cm}}{400 \text{ m}}$

Apply the Idea

8. To film a movie on Gulliver, the director uses a miniature model of the giant that is supposed to look 50 feet tall. If the model of Gulliver is 18 inches high, how high will a 10 inch model tree look?

Write About It

9. Explain how you can tell that this diagram of a 40-foot wide by 30-foot high building is *not* drawn to scale.

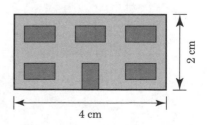

2 cm

4 cm

Chapter 5 Review

In this chapter, you have learned

- To understand and write ratios
- To use ratios and proportions
- To find the missing number in a proportion by cross-multiplying and dividing
- To solve proportions involving scale

Words You Know

From the lists of Words to Learn, choose the word or phrase that best completes each statement.

1. A ___ is a comparison of two numbers.

2. The ___ is the product of the numbers diagonally across from each other in a proportion.

3. A ___ is a drawing that shows a distance or an object in proportion to its real measurement.

4. Ratios that have the same value are called ___ .

5. A statement that two ratios are equal is a ___ .

6. A ___ is a ratio that compares the measurements in a drawing or model to the actual measurements.

More Practice *Show your work on a separate sheet of paper.*

Write a ratio for each comparison.

7. 3 hits for 10 at bats

8. 2 cans for $1.99

9. 55 miles in 1 hour

10. 2 inches for every 3 feet

Write the ratios described.

11. In a class there are 25 students. 15 are girls.
    a. What is the ratio of girls to total students?
    b. What is the ratio of boys to girls?

12. A jar contains 15 marbles. 7 are red, 5 are blue, and the rest are white.
    a. What is the ratio of blue marbles to red marbles?
    b. What is the ratio of red marbles to total marbles?
    c. What is the ratio of white marbles to total marbles?

13. One panel of a quilt has 4 green triangles and 6 white triangles.
    a. What is the ratio of white triangles to green triangles?
    b. What is the ratio of green triangles to total triangles?
    c. If there are 12 panels in the whole quilt, what is the equivalent ratio of white triangles to green triangles?

Tell whether each statement forms a true proportion.

14. $\frac{4}{6} = \frac{10}{15}$ 15. $\frac{10}{9} = \frac{30}{3}$ 16. $\frac{12}{36} = \frac{21}{63}$ 17. $\frac{12}{8} = \frac{15}{4}$

Find the missing number in each proportion.

18. $\frac{10}{?} = \frac{15}{3}$ 19. $\frac{4}{5} = \frac{?}{20}$ 20. $\frac{1.5}{2} = \frac{8}{?}$ 21. $\frac{?}{3} = \frac{.5}{2}$

Solve the following proportions involving map scale.

22. $\frac{2 \text{ in.}}{3 \text{ mi.}} = \frac{5 \text{ in.}}{? \text{ mi.}}$ 23. $\frac{1 \text{ cm}}{4 \text{ km}} = \frac{? \text{ cm}}{10 \text{ km}}$ 24. $\frac{1.5 \text{ cm}}{? \text{ m}} = \frac{6 \text{ cm}}{20 \text{ m}}$

Problems You Can Solve

25. Aaron takes 24 pictures of a school event and hands in 5 of them to the yearbook committee. He keeps the rest.
    a. What is the ratio of the pictures Aaron hands in to the pictures he takes?
    b. What is the ratio of the pictures he hands in to the pictures he keeps?

26. Kara, the yearbook art editor, can enlarge or reduce a photo to fit an available space, as long as the photo's measurements stay in proportion. Can she enlarge one of Aaron's 4-inch wide by 6-inch long photos to fit a 5-inch by 9-inch space without trimming it?

27. To fit a reduced version of Aaron's 4-inch wide by 6-inch long photo in a space that is 3 inches wide, how long must the space be?

28. To design the yearbook, Kara uses a special computer program that lets her view a whole page by reducing each page on a scale of 3 page inches:2 screen inches. If a page appears 8 inches wide on Kara's computer screen, how wide will it be in the yearbook?

29. If Kara has to include 3 photos for every 2 pages of the yearbook, how many photos will she need for a 180-page yearbook?

30. If Kara uses only 1 out of every 4 pictures the yearbook's photography team submits, how many photos does the team hand in?

Chapter 5 Practice Test

Write a ratio for each comparison.

1. 4 lemons for 1 pie

2. 12 eggs for 6 omelettes

3. 3 miles in 20 minutes

4. 300 words in 6 minutes

5. 25 people to 5 station wagons

6. 2 cups of water to 1 cup of rice

Answer each question with a ratio.

There are 352 students in the high school band. 190 are girls.

7. What is the ratio of girls to students in the band?

8. What is the ratio of girls to boys?

9. What is the ratio of students in the band to boys?

Tell whether each statement forms a true proportion.

10. $\frac{1}{2} = \frac{2}{3}$

11. $\frac{4}{6} = \frac{8}{12}$

12. $\frac{11}{22} = \frac{15}{30}$

Find the missing number in each proportion.

13. $\frac{3}{10} = \frac{?}{20}$

14. $\frac{5}{6} = \frac{?}{18}$

15. $\frac{12}{1} = \frac{?}{3}$

16. $\frac{48}{56} = \frac{6}{?}$

17. $\frac{?}{18} = \frac{90}{15}$

18. $\frac{17.6}{2.2} = \frac{8}{?}$

Solve.

19. A recipe calls for 4 cups of broth and 3 cups of vegetables. How many cups of vegetables will be needed for 24 cups of broth?

20. Yoshiko can read 25 pages in one hour. The book she is reading is 750 pages long. How long will it take her to read the book?

21. It took Tyrell 2 hours to ride his bike 28 miles. How far will he ride in 5 hours?

22. Marina finished 8 of the 32 potholders she is making. It took her 2 days to make 8. How long will it take her to make 32 potholders?

23. A summer camp has 5 counselors for every 15 children. How many counselors will there be if there are 60 children?

24. A model boat uses the scale 1 inch to 2 feet. If the sail on the model is 4 inches high, how high is the sail on the boat?

25. A map uses the scale .5 inches to 10 miles. If two towns are 25 miles apart, how far apart are they on the map?

Chapter 6
Percents

In this chapter, you will learn

- To write percents as fractions and decimals
- To write fractions and decimals as percents
- To find a percent of a number
- To find what percent a part is of a whole
- To find a number when you know a percent of it
- To use shortcuts with percents

Julie goes shopping for a new compact disc at Tune Town Music. Many of the signs she sees in the record store advertise sale prices. The discount, or amount of money off the regular price, is often written as a percent. Percents also are used to express parts of a whole.

What percent of the people surveyed think Tune Town has the best selection? A CD at Tune Town costs what fraction of the competition's price? How much will Julie save if she buys the Pure of Heart CD? Will it cost more or less than the Mike and Ike CD? What percent of the regular price will she save on the Mike and Ike CD? If Julie saves $3 on a CD that was marked 25% off, what was the original price of the CD?

In this chapter you will learn about percents and how to find the answers to these and other questions that come up in your daily life, especially when you shop or deal with money.

Buy at Tune Town and pay only 75% of the competition's price on every CD!

ALL CD's in this bin 25% off

NEW
Mike and Ike CD
Today Only—
$2.00 off

NEW
Pure of Heart CD
$15.00 reg. price
Now on Sale
10% off

4 out of 5 shoppers surveyed say Tune Town has the best selection in town.

6.1 Writing Percents

In This Lesson, You Will Learn
To write percents as fractions and decimals

Words to Learn
Percent a comparison of a number to 100
Ratio a comparison of two numbers

On the way home from school, Luis noticed a sign advertising a sale where shoppers could save 15% on a $100 jacket.

New Idea
Percent and the symbol % mean "for each 100" or "out of 100." A **percent** is a **ratio** or comparison of a number to 100. 15% reads "15 percent" and means 15 for each 100.

15 parts out of 100 parts are shaded.

15% of the whole is shaded.

15% can be written in other ways.

As a fraction: $\frac{15}{100}$ As a decimal: .15

$$\frac{part}{whole} = \frac{15}{100}$$

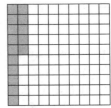

1 out of 100 parts is shaded.

1% of the whole is shaded.

As a fraction: $\frac{1}{100}$ As a decimal: .01

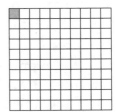

25 out of 100 parts are shaded.

25% of the whole is shaded.

As a fraction: $\frac{25}{100}$ As a decimal: .25

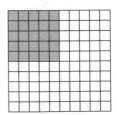

50 out of 100 parts are shaded.

50% of the whole is shaded.

As a fraction: $\frac{50}{100}$ As a decimal: .50

100 out of 100 parts are shaded.

100% of the whole is shaded.

All of the figure is shaded.

As a fraction: $\frac{100}{100}$ As a decimal: 1

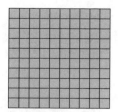

✓ Check Your Understanding

Write a fraction, decimal, and percent for the shaded part of the figure.

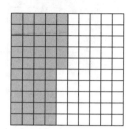

Focus on the Idea

A percent is a comparison of a number to 100. 25% means 25 for each 100, or $\frac{25}{100}$, or .25.

Practice *Show your work on a separate sheet of paper.*

1. Joe correctly answered 78 questions out of 100 on the test. What percent of the questions did he answer correctly?

2. There are 100 pennies in a dollar. What is 5% of one dollar?

3. According to Mike's phone bill, 8 out of every 100 calls this month were out-of-state calls. The rest were local calls.
   a. What percent of the calls were out-of-state calls?
   b. What percent of the calls were local calls?

Extend the Idea

By looking at pictures of percents you can write percents as decimals and fractions. You can also use the meaning of *percent* to write equivalent fractions and decimals.

Percent means "out of 100." So, to write a percent as a fraction, drop the % sign, make the percent the numerator and 100 the denominator. Write in lowest terms.

Example: Write 75% as a fraction.

Step 1: Remove the percent sign and write the percent as the numerator and 100 as the denominator.　　$\frac{75}{100}$

Step 2: To write in lowest terms, look for the greatest common factor. The greatest common factor of 75 and 100 is 25. Divide 75 and 100 by 25.

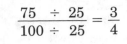

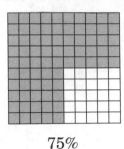 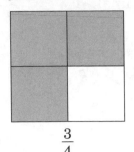

$$75\% \qquad = \qquad \frac{3}{4}$$

75% is equivalent to $\frac{3}{4}$.

A percent can be more than a whole.

Example: Write 125% as a fraction.

Step 1: Remove the percent sign and write the percent as the numerator and 100 as the denominator.

$$\frac{125}{100}$$

Step 2: If the result is an improper fraction, make it into a mixed number and write in lowest terms.

$$\frac{125}{100} = 1\frac{1}{4}$$

$$125\% = 1\frac{1}{4}$$

To write a percent as a decimal, drop the % sign and find the decimal point. If there is no decimal point, place it at the end of the number. Then move the decimal point 2 places to the left.

Example 1: Write 45% as a decimal.

Step 1: Remove the % sign and write the decimal point at the end.

45.

Step 2: Move the decimal point 2 places to the left.

.45

$$45\% = .45$$

Example 2: Write 5% as a decimal.

Step 1: Remove the % sign and write the decimal point at the end.

5.

Step 2: Move the decimal point 2 places to the left. Add a zero as a placeholder.

.05

$$5\% = .05$$

Example 3:   Write 115% as a decimal.

Step 1:   Remove the % sign and write the   115.
decimal point at the end.

Step 2:   Move the decimal point 2 places to   1.15
the left.

$$115\% = 1.15$$

✓ Check the Math

Joe reads about a survey in which 8% of students surveyed were in favor of a longer school day. In an essay about the survey, Joe wrote that .80 of the students surveyed were in favor of a longer school day. Is he correct? Explain your answer.

Practice   *Show your work on a separate sheet of paper.*

Write each percent as a decimal.

   4. 12%　　　**5.** 20%　　　**6.** 95%　　　**7.** 3%

   8. 50%　　　**9.** 88%　　　**10.** 9%　　　**11.** 135%

Write each percent as a fraction in lowest terms.

 12. 80%　　　**13.** 100%　　　**14.** 6%　　　**15.** 13%

 16. 35%　　　**17.** 78%　　　**18.** 1%　　　**19.** 120%

Apply the Idea

20.   Luis saw another sign for a store that was selling jackets at a 20% discount. What fraction of the price was discounted? Write your answer in lowest terms.

21.   25% of the charges on Jorge's MegaCharge Card were made at CD World Music. What fraction of his charges were made there? Write your answer in lowest terms.

22.   If 33% of every dollar spent on gasoline goes to transportation taxes, how many cents of each gas dollar is spent on taxes?

✎ Write About It

23.   Use a dictionary to find the meanings of the words *centimeter*, *centennial*, and *century*. What do their meanings have in common with *percent*?

➤ 6.2 Writing Fractions and Decimals as Percents

In This Lesson, You Will Learn
To write fractions as percents
To write decimals as percents

Jamie decides to save 1 out of every 4 dollars she earns working at the ice cream shop. What percent of her money does she save?

New Idea
To find the percent of money Jamie saves, write the ratio of the money she saves as a fraction.

1 out of 4 $\rightarrow \dfrac{1}{4}$

Change the ratio into a percent by finding an equivalent ratio with a denominator of 100. Set up a proportion. Cross multiply and divide to find the missing numbers.

$\dfrac{1}{4} \diagdown \dfrac{?}{100} \rightarrow 1 \times 100 = 100 \rightarrow 100 \div 4 = 25$

$\dfrac{1}{4} = \dfrac{25}{100} \rightarrow \dfrac{25}{100} = 25\%$

Jamie saves 25% of the money she earns.

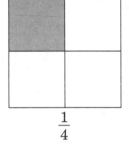

$\dfrac{1}{4}$

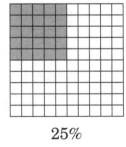

25%

You also can use what you know about fractions and decimals to change fractions to percents. Change the fraction to a decimal and then change the decimal to a percent.

Example: Write $\dfrac{3}{5}$ as a percent.

Step 1: Divide the numerator by the denominator.

$5\overline{)3.0}^{\,.6}$

Step 2: Write the decimal as a percent.

.6

Move the decimal point 2 places to the right. If necessary, add a zero to hold the place.

60.

Add a percent sign.

60%

$\dfrac{3}{5} = .6 = 60\%$

To change a mixed number to a percent, write the number as an improper fraction and follow the same steps.

Example: Write $1\frac{1}{2}$ as a percent.

  Step 1: Write the mixed number as an improper fraction.

$$1\frac{1}{2} = \frac{3}{2}$$

  Step 2: Divide the numerator by the denominator.

$$2\overline{)3.0}\quad\begin{array}{c}1.5\end{array}$$

  Step 3: Write the decimal as a percent. Move the decimal point 2 places to the right. Add a percent sign.

$$1.50 = 150\%$$

$$1\frac{1}{2} = 1.5 = 150\%$$

Focus on the Idea

To change any fraction to a percent, first make the fraction into a decimal by dividing the numerator by the denominator. Then write the decimal quotient as a percent. To write a decimal as a percent, move the decimal point 2 decimal places to the right and add a percent sign.

$$\frac{3}{5} = 3 \div 5 = .6 = 60\%$$

Practice *Show your work on a separate sheet of paper.*

Write each decimal as a percent.

1. .35   2. .6   3. .05   4. 1.35

Write each fraction as a percent. Round percents to the nearest tenth.

5. $\frac{1}{2}$ 6. $\frac{1}{3}$ 7. $\frac{3}{4}$ 8. $\frac{1}{5}$ 9. $\frac{2}{5}$

10. $\frac{2}{3}$ 11. $\frac{4}{5}$ 12. $1\frac{3}{4}$ 13. $\frac{1}{8}$ 14. $\frac{3}{8}$

Apply the Idea

15. The basketball shoes that Chris wants to buy are on sale at two different stores. The regular price is the same at both stores, but the shoes are 30% off at SportsWorld and $\frac{1}{4}$ off at Court King. Which store is offering the bigger discount? How do you know?

16. A company's profits rose $1\frac{1}{4}$ times. What percent did profits rise?

Write About It

17. Which one of these three does not belong with the others: $\frac{3}{4}$, .075, and 75%? Explain your answer.

↴ 6.3 Finding a Percent of a Number

In This Lesson, You Will Learn
To find a percent of a number

Marc is planning to buy a new TV. A local electronics store is having a 10% off sale on everything in the store. If $300 is the regular price of the model Marc wants to buy, how much money does he save if he buys the TV at 10% off?

New Idea

One way to figure out how much Marc saves is to think of the meaning of 10% as 10 for each 100. So Marc will save $10 for each $100 of the whole price. What does he save if the whole is $300?

$$\frac{part}{whole} = \frac{10}{100} = \frac{?}{300}$$

The 10% discount will save Marc $30 on a $300 TV.

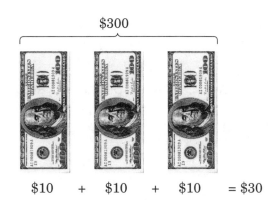

$$\$10 \quad + \quad \$10 \quad + \quad \$10 \quad = \$30$$

Marc was able to think of the whole (300) in groups of 100, but you cannot always do this. Another way to find the percent of a number is to use multiplication. Write the percent as a decimal and multiply where you see the word "of."

$$\begin{array}{cc} 10\% \text{ of} & 300 \text{ is } 30. \\ \downarrow & \downarrow \\ .10 & \times \ 300 = 30 \end{array}$$

Example 1: Find 15% of 60.

    Step 1: Write the decimal as a percent.   15% = .15

    Step 2: Multiply the two numbers.

$$\begin{array}{r} 60 \\ \times\ .15 \\ \hline 3\ 00 \\ 6\ 00 \\ \hline 9.00 \end{array}$$

    15% of 60 is 9.

Example 2: Find 130% of 90.

    Step 1: Write the percent as a decimal.   130% = 1.30

    Step 2: Multiply the two numbers.   1.3 × 90 = 117.0

    130% of 90 is 117.

Focus on the Idea

To find a percent of a number, write the percent as a decimal and multiply by the whole.

$$\frac{\%}{100} = \frac{?}{\text{whole}}$$

Practice *Show your work on a separate sheet of paper.*

Find the percent of each number.

1. 15% of 100
2. 25% of $80
3. 45% of 220

4. 30% of $500
5. 15% of 119
6. 20% of 65

7. 50% of 90
8. 5% of $170
9. 2% of 400

10. 12% of 75
11. 35% of 95
12. 18% of 60

Apply the Idea

13. The Bruins are offering a 10% discount on all tickets to this week's game. The regular price of a ticket is $15.
    a. How much money do buyers save on each ticket?
    b. How much does each discounted ticket cost?

14. Diane and Adriana go shopping together for leather jackets. Diane buys a $195 jacket that is on sale for 20% off. Adriana chooses a $225 jacket that is discounted 25%.
    a. Who saves more money on her jacket?
    b. Who pays more for her jacket?

15. Of 50 people surveyed, 80% said they exercised only once a week. 20% said they work out every day.
    a. What number of people surveyed exercise only once a week?
    b. How many people work out every day?

16. On a recent 25-question test, Dean answered 84% of the questions correctly.
    a. How many did he answer correctly?
    b. How many did he answer incorrectly?

Write About It

17. Would you rather have a coupon good for 10% off or $10 off an item that costs $50? Which would you rather have on an item that costs $100? An item that costs $150? Explain your answers.

6.4 Writing a Part as a Percent

In This Lesson, You Will Learn
To find what percent a part is of a whole

Josh wants to buy a portable CD player. The model he wants costs $120, but he buys it on sale for $30 off. What percent of the regular price does he save?

New Idea
Josh knows the part (30) and whole (120). He wants to find the equivalent percent.

$$\frac{\text{part}}{\text{whole}} = \frac{?}{100} = \frac{30}{120}$$

To find the equivalent percent, write the part and whole as a fraction with the part as the numerator and the whole as the denominator. Then, change the fraction to a decimal by dividing the numerator by the denominator. Write the decimal as a percent.

$$\frac{30}{120} \rightarrow 120\overline{)30.00}^{.25} \rightarrow .25 = 25\%$$

$30 is 25% of $120, so Josh saves 25%.

Example:	10 is what percent of 60?	
Step 1:	Write a fraction with the part as the numerator and the whole as the denominator.	$\frac{\text{part}}{\text{whole}} = \frac{10}{60}$
Step 2:	Divide the numerator by the denominator.	$60\overline{)10.0000}^{.1666}$
	Round to 3 decimal places.	.167
Step 3:	Write the decimal as a percent.	.167 = 16.7%
	10 is 16.7% of 60.	

A percent may be bigger than a whole.

Example:	45 is what percent of 30?	
Step 1:	Write a fraction with the part as the numerator and the whole as the denominator.	$\frac{\text{part}}{\text{whole}} = \frac{45}{30}$

Step 2:	Divide the numerator by the denominator.	$\dfrac{1.5}{30\overline{)450}}$
Step 3:	Write the decimal as a percent. 45 is 150% of 30.	$1.50 = 150\%$

Focus on the Idea

To find what percent a part is of a whole, write a fraction with the part as the numerator and the whole as the denominator. Change the fraction to a decimal by dividing the numerator by the denominator. Write the decimal as a percent.

Practice *Show your work on a separate sheet of paper.*
Find the percent using the part and whole.

1. What percent is 40 of 100?

2. What percent is 30 of 50?

3. What percent is 15 of 60?

4. 45 is what percent of 135?

5. 15 is what percent of 75?

6. 42 is what percent of 60?

7. 30 is what percent of 24?

8. 6 is what percent of 200?

9. 52 is what percent of 80?

10. .25 is what percent of 2?

Apply the Idea

11. A jacket that usually sells for $30 is on sale for $6 off.
    a. What is the percent of savings?
    b. What is the sale price?

12. Joe bought $3 worth of baseball trading cards and paid $.15 tax. What is the percent tax?

13. Helena ran 33 meters of the 220-meter race before she twisted her ankle and had to withdraw from the race. What percent of the race did she complete?

Write About It

14. In a 10-day period, it rains 3 days. What percent of the days does it rain? What percent of the days does it not rain? What happens if you add the two percents? What does this percent mean?

6.5 Finding the Original Number When a Percent of It Is Known

In This Lesson, You Will Learn

To find a number when you know a percent of it

Max is planning a vacation in Florida. Just before he makes his reservations, he reads that his hotel has already raised its room rate by $12, a 5% increase after only six months in business. What was the original room rate Max would have paid if he had reserved his room earlier?

New Idea

Max needs to find the number of which 5% is 12. In this case, you know the percent (5) and the part (12), and you need to find the original number (the whole).

$$\frac{\text{part}}{\text{whole}} = \frac{5}{100} = \frac{12}{?}$$

To find the original number, write the percent as a decimal and divide the part by the decimal.

$$5\% \rightarrow .05$$

$$
\begin{array}{r}
240 \\
05\,)\overline{1200} \\
-\ 10 \\
\hline
20 \\
-\ 20 \\
\hline
00
\end{array}
$$

12 is 5% of 240, so the original room rate was $240.

Example 1: 80 is 20% of what number?

    Step 1: Write the percent as a decimal.

    Step 2: Divide the part by the decimal.

        80 is 20% of 400.

$$20\% = .20$$

$$
\begin{array}{r}
400 \\
20\,)\overline{8000}
\end{array}
$$

Example 2: 300 is 150% of what number?

    Step 1: Write the percent as a decimal.

    Step 2: Divide the part by the decimal.

        300 is 150% of 200.

$$150\% = 1.5$$

$$
\begin{array}{r}
200 \\
15\,)\overline{3000}
\end{array}
$$

Focus on the Idea

To find the original number when a percent of it is known, write the percent as a decimal, and divide the part by the decimal.

Practice *Show your work on a separate sheet of paper.*
Find the original number.

1. 20 is 30% of what number?

2. 50% of what number is 13?

3. 25% of what number is 12?

4. 7% of what number is 1.4?

5. 100% of what number is 96?

6. 34 is 10% of what number?

7. 75 is 75% of what number?

8. 50 is 20% of what number?

9. 12 is 15% of what number?

10. 120% of what number is 72?

Apply the Idea

11. Susan scored 5 goals in one game. This was 25% of her season total. What was her season total?

12. A bank pays 5% interest per year for savings accounts. How much do you need in savings to earn $100 interest in a year?

13. A sign for a pair of shoes reads "20% off! Save $12!" What is the original price of the shoes?

14. The price of oil rose 2%, or $.50 per barrel, last year. How much did a barrel cost before the increase?

15. Joan is a salesperson for a book company. She earns 7% commission on her total sales. Last year she earned $1,400 in commissions. What were her total sales?

16. Lucy earned $450 in December. Her pay stub indicated that this was 120% of what she earned in November. How much did she earn in November?

Write About It

17. Think of two different situations where you might use percents. Create two different word problems and explain how to solve them.

6.6 Using Shortcuts with Percents

In This Lesson, You Will Learn
To use shortcuts with percents

Andy is shopping in a store. A $28 shirt is marked 25% off. How can he find out how much he will save without pencil and paper or a calculator?

New Idea

There are many quick ways to find certain percents. One way is to think of an equivalent fraction that is easier to use.

Andy uses $\frac{1}{4}$ for 25%. Multiplying by $\frac{1}{4}$ is the same as dividing by 4.

$$25\% \text{ of } 28 \to \frac{1}{4} \text{ of } 28 \to 28 \div 4 = 7$$

25% of $28 is $7. Andy saves $7.

50%	$= \frac{1}{2}$
25%	$= \frac{1}{4}$
20%	$= \frac{1}{5}$
12.5%	$= \frac{1}{8}$

Example: Find 20% of 40.

Step 1: Find an equivalent fraction. $\qquad 20\% = \frac{1}{5}$

Step 2: To find $\frac{1}{5}$, divide by 5. $\qquad 40 \div 5 = 8$

20% of 40 is 8.

The following method works well if you want to estimate a percent.

Example: Estimate 25% of $318.99.

Step 1: Find an equivalent fraction.

Step 2: Round 318.99 to a whole number that is easily divisible by 4. $\qquad 25\% = \frac{1}{4}$

318.99 rounds up to 320

Step 3: To find $\frac{1}{4}$, divide by 4.

25% of $318.99 is about $80. $\qquad 320 \div 4 = 80$

Here is a method to find multiples of 20% or 25%.

Example: Find 75% of 80.

Step 1: Find an equivalent fraction to 75%. $\qquad 75\% = \frac{3}{4}$

Step 2: Think of $\frac{3}{4}$ as a multiple of $\frac{1}{4}$. $\qquad \frac{3}{4} = 3 \times \frac{1}{4}$

Step 3: To find $\frac{1}{4}$, divide by 4. $\qquad 80 \div 4 = 20$

Step 4: To find $\frac{3}{4}$, multiply by 3. $\qquad 3 \times 20 = 60$

75% of 80 is 60.

You can find 10% of any number by moving the decimal point 1 place to the left.

Example: Find 10% of 315.

Move the decimal point 1 place to the left. $315 \rightarrow 31.5$

10% of 315 is 31.5.

5% is $\frac{1}{2}$ of 10%, so a quick way to find 5% is to find 10% and then find $\frac{1}{2}$ of that number.

Example: Find 5% of 320.

Step 1: Find 10%. Move the decimal point one place to the left. $320 \rightarrow 32$

Step 2: Find $\frac{1}{2}$ of 32. Divide by 2. $32 \div 2 = 16$

5% of 320 is 16.

Find multiples of 5% by combining 10% and 5%.

Example: Find 15% of 25.

Step 1: Think of 15% as 10% + 5%.

Step 2: Find 10%. Move the decimal point one place to the left. $25 \rightarrow 2.5$

Step 3: Find 5%. Take $\frac{1}{2}$ of 10%. $2.5 \div 2 = 1.25$

Step 4: Add 10% and 5%. $2.5 + 1.25 = 3.75$

15% of 25 is 3.75.

Focus on the Idea
To mentally calculate percents, use a simpler equivalent fraction, or think of the percent in groups of 10% and 5%.

Practice *Show your work on a separate sheet of paper.*
Solve.

1. Find 20% of $350.
2. Find 10% of 49.
3. Find 15% of 44.
4. Find 25% of 60.
5. Find 40% of 75.
6. Find 50% of 225.

Apply the Idea
Estimate the percent.

7. A $88 tennis racket is on sale for 20% off. About how much will a customer save?

8. About how much interest will $275 earn in a year at an interest rate of 5% a year?

Write About It

9. Explain two ways you could find 30% of a number.

In this chapter, you have learned

- To write percents as fractions and decimals
- To write fractions and decimals as percents
- To find a percent of a number
- To find what percent a part is of a whole
- To find a number when you know a percent of it
- To use shortcuts with percents

Words You Know

1. Use the word *ratio* to write a sentence to define the word *percent*.

More Practice *Show your work on a separate sheet of paper.*

Write a percent for each ratio.

2. $\dfrac{3}{100}$

3. $\dfrac{75}{100}$

4. 22:100

Write a percent for each decimal.

5. .45

6. .6

7. .05

Copy and complete the chart. Write fractions in lowest terms.

	Percent	Fraction
8.	50%	?
9.	25%	?
10.	?	$\dfrac{3}{4}$
11.	?	$\dfrac{1}{5}$
12.	?	$\dfrac{2}{5}$
13.	60%	?
14.	80%	?
15.	?	$\dfrac{1}{3}$
16.	?	$\dfrac{1}{8}$

Find the percent of each number.

17. What is 15% of 90?

18. What is 30% of 150?

19. What is 22% of 95?

20. What is 35% of 80?

Find the percent the part is of the whole.

21. What percent is 15 of 60?

22. What percent is 11 of 55?

23. 24 is what percent of 72?

24. What percent is 30 of 30?

Find the original number.

25. 10 is 40% of what number?

26. 45 is 75% of what number?

27. 32 is 100% of what number?

28. 16 is 5% of what number?

Solve.

29. What percent is 20 of 30?

30. What is 70% of 34?

31. What is 100% of 38?

32. 12 is 8% of what number?

33. What percent is 5 of 50?

34. What is 15% of 62?

35. 16 is 8% of what number?

36. What percent is 12 of 36?

37. What percent is 75 of 50?

38. What is 110% of 45?

Problems You Can Solve

39. If 4 out of 5 people surveyed think Tune Town Music has the best selection in town, what percent think the store's selection is best?

40. If a CD at Tune Town costs 75% of what the competition charges, a Tune Town CD costs what fraction of the competition's price?

41. How much money will Julie save if she buys the $15 Pure of Heart CD for 10% off?

42. Which costs more: the $15 Pure of Heart CD at 10% off, or the $16 Mike and Ike CD on sale for $2 off?

43. What percent of the regular price will Julie save on the Mike and Ike CD?

44. If Julie saves $3 on a CD that was marked 25% off, what was the original price of the CD?

45. Julie's goal was to save $500 this year. She saved 110% of her goal. How much did she save?

Write a percent for each ratio.

1. 45:100

2. $\frac{5}{100}$

3. $\frac{28}{100}$

4. 33 to 100

Write each decimal as a percent.

5. .55

6. .09

7. .7

8. 1.00

Write each fraction as a percent.

9. $\frac{1}{4}$

10. $\frac{3}{5}$

11. $\frac{2}{3}$

12. $\frac{2}{8}$

Find the percent of each number.

13. What is 35% of 70?

14. What is 100% of 49?

15. What is 3% of 200?

16. What is 48% of 25?

Find the percent the part is of the whole.

17. What percent is 20 of 80?

18. What percent is 45 of 72?

19. 14 is what percent of 56?

20. What percent is 9 of 10?

Find the original number.

21. 12 is 60% of what number?

22. 50 is 25% of what number?

23. 18 is 15% of what number?

24. 3 is 8% of what number?

Solve.

25. What percent is 13 of 36?

26. 18 is 10% of what number?

27. What is 13% of 20?

28. What percent is 15 of 90?

29. What is 65% of 120?

30. 12 is 90% of what number?

31. What percent is 62 of 100?

32. 20 is 45% of what number?

Solve.

33. Jenna and Mariah's father tells them that he will give $10 to whomever has saved a larger percent of her salary at the end of the month. Jenna saves $54 of her $270 salary, and Mariah saves 25% of her $156 salary.

    a. Which one saves the larger percent of her salary?

    b. How much money does Mariah save?

34. Edward and Will bought the same pair of hiking boots, but Edward got his boots on sale for $39. If Edward paid only 60% of what Will paid, how much did Will's boots cost?

Chapter 7
Geometry

In this chapter, you will learn

- To indentify various polygons
- To find the perimeter of polygons
- To find the area of rectangles, squares, and other parallelograms
- To find the area of triangles
- To find the circumference of circles
- To find the area of circles
- To find the area of irregular figures
- To find the surface area of three-dimensional figures
- To find the volume of three-dimensional figures

House painters, gardeners, landscapers, dressmakers, ecologists, engineers, and park directors are examples of people who need to use geometric measurement in their work.

This is a diagram of Friendship Park, a recreation area. It shows the dimensions of the park and the various areas within the park.

If you wanted to put a fence around the Picnic Space, how much fencing would you need? How much space do the Hiking Trails take up? How would you find out whether the area of the Boating Lake is greater than the area of the Playing Field? How long is the track that goes around the Boating Lake?

In this chapter you will learn about geometric measurement as it applies to the real world.

Friendship Park

Playing Field

Picnic Space

1.5 km

2 km

1 km

8 km

7 km

4 km

5 km

1.5 km

Hiking Trails

Boating Lake

3 km

9 km

Identifying Polygons and Finding Their Perimeters

In This Lesson, You Will Learn

To identify various polygons
To find the perimeter of polygons

Words to Learn

Polygon a straight-sided, closed, two-dimensional figure with three or more sides. A two-dimensional figure is flat; you can measure it in only two directions.

Perimeter the distance around a figure

Parallel lines lines that extend in the same direction and are always the same distance apart

Parallelogram a 4-sided polygon whose opposite sides are parallel

Rectangle a parallelogram with 4 right angles

Right angle an angle that measures 90°

Square a rectangle with 4 equal sides

Triangle a polygon with 3 sides

The director of Friendship Park wants to fence in several sections of the park. To determine how much fencing she will need, she has to find the distance around the section she wants to fence.

New Idea

Friendship Park and several of its sections are **polygons**, or straight-sided, closed geometric figures that have at least three sides. The distance around a polygon is called its **perimeter**. You find the perimeter of a polygon by adding the lengths of its sides. Adding the measures of the sides always gives you the perimeter.

Friendship Park is a **parallelogram**, a 4-sided polygon whose opposite sides are **parallel lines**.

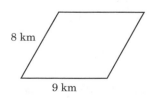

Example: Find the perimeter of Friendship Park. Add the measures of the sides. Pairs of opposite sides are equal.

The perimeter is 34 kilometers.

$8 + 8 + 9 + 9 = 34$

The Picnic Space is a **rectangle**, a parallelogram with 4 **right angles**. These are examples of right angles.

Example: Find the perimeter of the Picnic Space. Add the measures of the sides. Pairs of opposite sides are equal.

1 km

2 km

The perimeter is 6 kilometers.

$1 + 1 + 2 + 2 = 6$

The Playing Field is a **square**, a rectangle with 4 equal sides.

Example: Find the perimeter of the Playing Field. Add the measures of the sides. All sides are equal in a square

1.5 km

The perimeter is 6 kilometers.

$1.5 + 1.5 + 1.5 + 1.5 = 6$

The Hiking Trails section is a **triangle**, a polygon with 3 sides.

Example: Find the perimeter of the Hiking Trails section. Add the measures of the sides. A triangle has three sides.

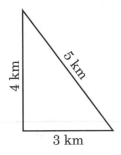

4 km

5 km

3 km

The perimeter is 12 kilometers.

$4 + 5 + 3 = 12$

Focus on the Idea

To find the perimeter of a polygon, add the measures of its sides.

Practice *Show your work on a separate sheet of paper.*

Find the perimeter of each figure.

1.
6 cm
5 cm

2. 2 ft
7 ft

3.
6 m
10 m
8 m

4. 3.5 mm   3.5 mm
5.2 mm

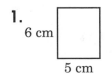

5.
42 cm
18 cm   18 cm
13 cm

6. 4.5 m   4.5 m
4.5 m   4.5 m
4.5 m

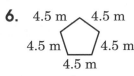

7.
3 cm
3 cm   3 cm
3 cm   3 cm
3 cm

8.
3 m
2 m   4 m
8.5 m   5 m

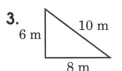

Apply the Idea

9. A 95-meter by 45-meter rectangle of grass in the Playing Field is set aside for soccer. How many meters of chalk striping are needed to outline the soccer field?

Write About It

10. Explain how the rule for finding the perimeter of a polygon can help you calculate how far a player runs when he touches every base after hitting a home run.

7.2 Finding the Area of Parallelograms

In This Lesson, You Will Learn

To find the area of rectangles, squares, and other parallelograms

Words to Learn

Area the amount of surface a figure covers

Square units area is measured in square units, such as square inches, square meters, and square miles

Base a side of a polygon

Height the distance between the base and the opposite side. The height makes a right angle with the base.

Formula a rule for solving a problem

Ms. Francis is planning to pave a small rectangular playground that is 4 meters long and 3 meters wide. She needs to know how much ground the playground covers. How can she calculate the size of the playground's surface?

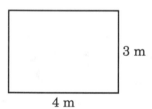

New Idea

Ms. Francis must find the **area** of the playground. Think of area as the number of squares needed to cover a figure. You can count 12 squares, so the area is 12 square meters, or 12 m². We call this kind of measurement **square units**.

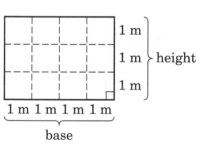

You can also find the area by multiplying the base by the **height**. The height is the distance between a particular side or **base** and its opposite side. The height always makes a right angle with the base.

Area of a rectangle = base × height

$$A = b \times h \quad \leftarrow \text{ Formula} \quad b = \text{base}, \ h = \text{height}$$

In the playground above, $b = 4$ and $h = 3$. $4 \times 3 = 12$.
The area of the playground is 12 square meters or $12\,m^2$.

You can find the area of any parallelogram by multiplying base × height.

In the rectangle, one of the sides gives you the height. In some parallelograms, the height is not one of the sides. You have to know the height. The height is a line drawn at a right angle to the base.

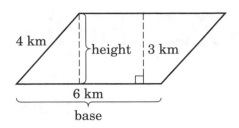

Example: Find the area of the parallelogram.

Step 1: Write the formula for area. $A = b \times h$

Step 2: Replace b with 6 and h with 3. $A = 6 \times 3$

Step 3: Multiply to find the area. $A = 18$

The area of the parallelogram is 18 square kilometers, or 18 km^2.

Focus on the Idea

To find the area of a rectangle, a square, or other parallelogram, multiply base × height. Be sure to label the answer in square units.

$A = b \times h$

Practice *Show your work on a separate sheet of paper.*

Find the area of each figure. You may want to use a calculator.

1.
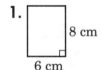
8 cm
6 cm

2.

4 ft
4 ft

3.

7 m
2 m

4.
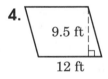
9.5 ft
12 ft

Find the area of each figure. You may want to use a calculator.

5. rectangle
base = 5 inches
height = 10 inches

6. square
side = 6 centimeters

7. parallelogram
base = 2 feet
height = 5.5 feet

Apply the Idea

8. A new basketball court is being built in Friendship Park. It will measure 84 feet by 50 feet. The basketball court will have to be properly surfaced. This will cost $3.50 per square foot. What will this job cost?

Write About It

9. Find out the official dimensions of a standard football field. Draw a diagram and calculate the area. Write about how you found the dimensions and calculated the area.

7.3 Finding the Area of Triangles

In This Lesson, You Will Learn

To find the area of triangles

Words to Learn

Altitude height

The town of Willis is approximately in the shape of a parallelogram. The town is building a bike path that will run straight from one corner of the town to the opposite corner. The path will cut the town into two halves. What is the area of each of the triangles created by the new bike path?

New Idea

The bike path divides the town in half, forming two equal triangles. Each triangle is half the size of the parallelogram, but each has the same base and height as the parallelogram. The height is sometimes called the **altitude**.

You can find the area of a parallelogram by multiplying base × height. The triangle is half the size of the parallelogram, so the area of the triangle is half the area of the parallelogram, or $\frac{1}{2}$ × base × height.

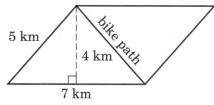

Area = base × height

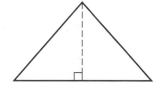

The area of the triangle is $\frac{1}{2}$ of the parallelogram.

Area of a triangle $= \frac{1}{2}$ × base × height

$$A = \frac{1}{2} \times b \times h$$ Formula for area of a triangle

$$A = \frac{1}{2} \times 28$$ Area of the town is $4 \times 7 = 28$ km^2.

$$A = 14$$

The area of this triangle is 14 km^2.   Remember to label square units.

You can use the formula $A = \frac{1}{2} \times b \times h$ to find the area of any triangle. Sometimes the height of a triangle is one of its sides.

Example: Find the area of the triangle.

Step 1: Write the formula for area of a triangle.

$$A = \frac{1}{2} \times b \times h$$

Step 2: Replace b with 1.5 and h with 2.

$$A = \frac{1}{2} \times 1.5 \times 2$$

Step 3: Multiply to find the area.

$$A = 1.5$$

The area of the triangle is 1.5 ft^2.

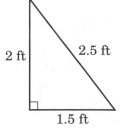

In some cases, you need to go outside a triangle to measure its height.

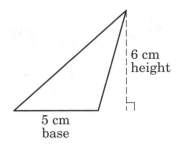
6 cm
height

5 cm
base

Example: Find the area of the triangle.

Step 1: Write the formula for area of a triangle.

$$A = \frac{1}{2} \times b \times h$$

Step 2: Replace b with 5 and h with 6.

$$A = \frac{1}{2} \times 5 \times 6$$

Step 3: Multiply to find the area.

$$A = 15$$

The area of the triangle is 15 cm².

Focus on the Idea

To calculate the area of a triangle, multiply $\frac{1}{2}$ × base × height.

$$A = \frac{1}{2} \times b \times h$$

Practice *Show your work on a separate sheet of paper.*

Find the area of each figure.

1.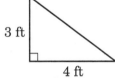
3 ft
4 ft

2.
8 m
10 m

3.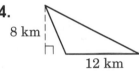
5 cm
15 cm

4.
8 km
12 km

5. triangle
base = 8 millimeters
height = 6 millimeters

6. square
side = 9 centimeters

7. parallelogram
base = 2.75 feet
height = 5.5 feet

Apply the Idea

8. To mark the bike path, volunteers are making foil pennants like the one shown at the right. How much foil, in square feet, is needed to cover one side of each pennant?

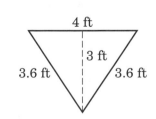
4 ft
3 ft
3.6 ft   3.6 ft

Write About It

9. Fold a piece of notebook paper and make a triangle. Measure that triangle and then calculate its area. Write about how you identified the measurements for the base and the height.

7.4 Finding the Circumference of Circles

In This Lesson, You Will Learn
To find the circumference of a circle

Words to Learn
Circle a set of points that are all the same distance from a given point, called the center

Circumference the distance around a circle

Diameter a line that passes through the center of the circle and has both its ends on the circle

Pi (π) the ratio of the circumference of a circle to its diameter. The ratio is the same for all circles: π is approximately 3.14.

A landscaper is designing a circular garden. A rope fence will enclose the garden. How much rope is needed to cover the distance around the garden?

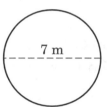

7 m

New Idea
The distance around a **circle** is called the **circumference**. There is a special relationship between the circumference of a circle and its **diameter**, a line that passes through the center of the circle. The ratio of the circumference to the diameter is the same for all circles. This ratio is represented by the Greek letter π **(pi)**.

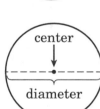

center

diameter

π has an infinite number of decimal places. It is usually rounded to 3.14. When you replace π with its approximate value of 3.14, use $\approx$ (approximately equal) instead of $=$ in the formula.

You can use this relationship to find the circumference of a circle if you know the diameter of the circle.

   Circumference $= \pi \times$ diameter

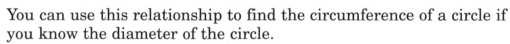

   $\qquad C = \pi \times d \quad \leftarrow$ Formula for circumference

The diameter of the garden is 7 meters, so $d = 7$.

$$C = \pi \times 7$$

Replace π with 3.14.　　$C \approx 3.14 \times 7$　　Remember to use $\approx$ with 3.14.

$$C \approx 21.98$$　　21.98 is very close to 22.

The distance around the garden is about 22 meters.

Example: Find the circumference of a circle whose diameter is 15 inches.

Step 1: Write the formula for circumference. $C = \pi \times d$

Step 2: Replace π with 3.14 and d with 15. $C \approx 3.14 \times 15$

Step 3: Multiply to find C. $C \approx 47.10$

The circumference of the circle is about 47.10 inches.

 You can use calculator keys to make solving the problem easier. Some calculators have a special ⬚π⬚ key that you can use instead of entering 3.14. To find $C = \pi \times 15$ using a calculator:

⬚π⬚ ⬚×⬚ 15 ⬚=⬚ 47.123890   Round your answer to the nearest hundredth.

The circumference is about 47.12 inches.

The answer you get using the ⬚π⬚ key will be more exact than the one you get using 3.14. You usually can round the answer to the nearest hundredth.

Focus on the Idea

To find the circumference of a circle, multiply the diameter by π.

$C = \pi \times d$

 Practice *Show your work on a separate sheet of paper.*

Find the circumference of each circle. Use 3.14 or the ⬚π⬚ key on your calculator. Round the answer to the nearest hundredth.

1. 5 cm

2. 8 ft

3. 12 m

4. 34 in.

5. diameter = 25 inches   6. diameter = 17.6 feet   7. diameter = 44 centimeters

Apply the Idea

8. A large party is being thrown in a circular tent. The tent has a diameter of 150 meters. If the host wants to hang a long string of white lights around the circumference of the tent, how many meters of lights are needed?

Entertainment Tent

Write About It

9. How would the circumference of a circle change if the diameter were doubled? Use any diameter to find the answer. Explain your answer.

7.5 Finding the Area of Circles

In This Lesson, You Will Learn

To find the area of circles

Words to Learn

Radius a line with one endpoint at the center of a circle and the other endpoint on the circle

Radii the plural form of radius

r^2 means radius × radius. It does *not* mean radius × 2.

A town gardener wants to plant flowers in the town's traffic circle. She needs to order one plant for every square foot of garden. If the diameter of the garden is 10 feet, how can she calculate the size of the circular garden in square feet?

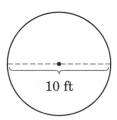

New Idea

The gardener needs to find the area of a circle. The **radius** of a circle is any line from the center of the circle to the edge of the circle. You can find the area of a circle by multiplying π × radius × radius.

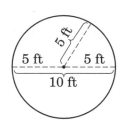

$$\text{Area} = \pi \times \text{radius} \times \text{radius}$$
$$A = \pi \times r \times r = \pi \times r^2 \quad \leftarrow \text{ Formula for area of a circle}$$

Two **radii** end-to-end are the same length as the diameter of the circle. The radius is half the diameter, or diameter ÷ 2. If the diameter of the circle is 10 feet, the radius is 10 ÷ 2 or 5 feet.

$$A = \pi \times r \times r$$

Replace π with 3.14 and r with 5.
$$A \approx 3.14 \times 5 \times 5$$
$$A \approx 78.5$$

The area of the traffic circle is about 78.5 ft². Remember to express your answer in square units.

Example: Find the area of a circle with a radius of 3 centimeters.

Step 1: Write the formula for the area of a circle. $A = \pi \times r \times r$

Step 2: Replace π with 3.14 and r with 3. $A \approx 3.14 \times 3 \times 3$

Step 3: Multiply. $A \approx 28.26$

The area of the circle is about 28.26 cm².

You can use calculator keys to make solving a problem easier.
To find $A = \pi \times r \times r$ using a calculator:

| π | | ⊠ | 5 | ⊠ | 5 | ▤ | 78.539816 |

The area is about 78.54 ft².

Remember to label your answer in square units. The answer you get is more exact than the one you get using 3.14. You can usually round the answer to the nearest hundredth.

Focus on the Idea

To find the area of a circle, multiply $\pi \times$ radius $\times$ radius.

$$A = \pi \times r \times r \quad or \quad A = \pi \times r^2$$

You can find the radius of a circle by dividing its diameter by 2.

 Practice *Show your work on a separate sheet of paper.*

Find the area of each circle. Use 3.14 or the π key on your calculator. Round the answer to the nearest hundredth.

1. 5.1 yd
2. 14.6 m
3. 96 ft
4. 8 mi.

5. 1 cm
6. 26 in.
7. 79 yd
8. 8.2 mm

Find the area of each circle. Use 3.14 or the π key on your calculator. Round the answer to the nearest hundredth.

9. radius = 6.8 centimeters
10. diameter = 5.6 inches
11. radius = 1.31 meters

Apply the Idea

12. A sprinkler can spray a fine mist over a circular region with a radius of 15 meters. How large an area can the sprinkler water?

13. A round wooden canopy has a diameter of 18 feet. With the sun directly overhead, about how many square feet of shade will the canopy provide?

Write About It

14. Imagine you are having a round glass tabletop made for a table in your home. If the diameter of the table is 4 feet and the glass costs $10 a square foot, how much money will the tabletop cost? Explain how you found the answer.

7.6 Finding the Area of Irregular Figures

In This Lesson, You Will learn
To find the area of irregular figures

Words to Learn
Irregular figure any shape that can be broken up into other recognizable shapes

A circular flower garden with a radius of 4 feet sits in a rectangular grass field that measures 30 feet by 15 feet. The landscaper wants to fertilize the grass. To buy the fertilizer, he has to know the number of square feet, or area, covered with grass. How can he find the area of the grass region of the field?

New Idea
The grass field is an **irregular figure**. You can find the area of an irregular shape like this one by subtracting the area of the smaller familiar shape (circle) from the larger familiar shape (a rectangle).

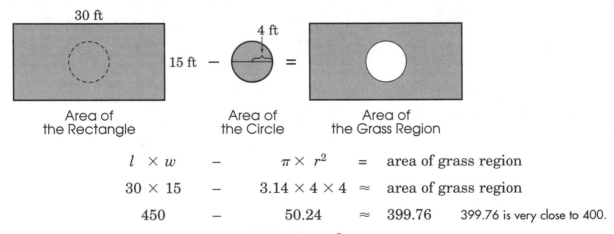

Area of the Rectangle — Area of the Circle = Area of the Grass Region

$l \times w$	—	$\pi \times r^2$	=	area of grass region
30×15	—	$3.14 \times 4 \times 4$	$\approx$	area of grass region
450	—	50.24	$\approx$	399.76 399.76 is very close to 400.

The area of the grass region is about 400 ft^2.

Some irregular shapes can be broken into two or more familiar shapes. You can find the area of these types of irregular shapes by finding and then adding the areas of the familiar shapes.

Example: Find the area of the irregular figure.

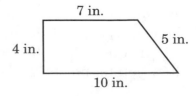

Step 1: Draw a line dividing the figure into two familiar shapes: a rectangle and a triangle. The height of the rectangle is also the height of the triangle.

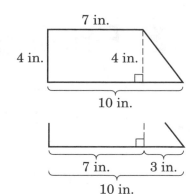

Step 2: Find the base of the triangle. Subtract the smaller measurement from the bigger one: 10 in. − 7 in. = 3 in.

Step 3: Find the area of the rectangle.

$$A = b \times h$$
$$A = 7 \times 4 = 28$$

Step 4: Find the area of the triangle.

$$A = \frac{1}{2} \times b \times h$$
$$A = \frac{1}{2} \times 3 \times 4 = 6$$

Step 5: Add the areas of the two shapes. The area of the figure is 34 in.².

$$28 + 6 = 34$$

Focus on the Idea

To find the area of an irregular figure, first identify the familiar shapes within it and find the area of each. If the irregular shape contains familiar shapes, subtract the areas of the smaller familiar shapes from the area of the largest. If the irregular shape can be broken into familiar shapes, add the areas of the familiar shapes.

Practice *Show your work on a separate sheet of paper.*

Find the area of the shaded region. You may want to use a calculator. Round any decimals to the nearest tenth.

1.
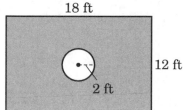

2.
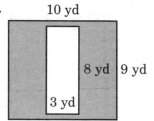

3.
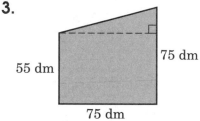

 Apply the Idea

4. A pool director wants to cover the deck surrounding the adult and children's swimming pools with a layer of rubber treading to prevent people from slipping. How many square feet will be covered?

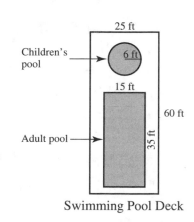

 Write About It

5. Design and draw your own irregular figure. Label the dimensions and find the area.

In This Lesson, You Will Learn

To find the surface area of three-dimensional figures

Words to Learn

Rectangular prism a three-dimensional figure with 6 rectangles for sides

Three-dimensional having length, width, and height. Most objects in real life are three-dimensional.

Faces the flat surfaces or sides of a prism

Surface area the total area of the sides of a three-dimensional figure

Edge a line where two sides of a prism meet

Lynn is painting a rectangular storage box. The box is 4 feet long, 3 feet wide, and 2 feet high. In order to calculate how much paint she needs, Lynn needs to find the total area of all 6 sides of the box.

New Idea

The storage box is in the shape of a **rectangular prism**, a **three-dimensional** figure with 6 rectangles for sides, called **faces**. The total area of all 6 faces is called the **surface area**. A line where two sides meet is called an **edge**.

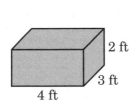

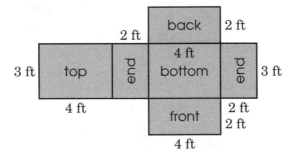

By looking at the flattened view of the box, you can see all 6 rectangular faces. Each pair of opposite faces has the same size. To find the surface area, first find the area of each face and then find the sum of all 6 areas.

top and bottom	4 feet × 3 feet	12 ft² each
front and back	4 feet × 2 feet	8 ft² each
ends	3 feet × 2 feet	6 ft² each

Total surface area = 12 + 12 + 8 + 8 + 6 + 6 = 52 ft²

The surface area of the storage box is 52 ft².

A cube is a prism with 6 squares of equal size for faces. All of the edges have the same length. To find the surface area, find the area of one face and multiply by 6.

Example: Find the surface area of a cube with an edge of 5 inches.

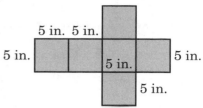

Step 1: Draw a picture of the cube.

Step 2: Find the area of one face.   5 in. × 5 in. = 25 in.²

Step 3: Multiply the area by 6.   6 × 25 in.² = 150 in.²

The surface area of the cube is 150 in².

Focus on the Idea

To find surface area of a rectangular prism, find the sum of the areas of all the faces. To find the surface area of a cube, find the area of one face and multiply by 6.

Practice *Show your work on a separate sheet of paper.*

Find the surface area of each figure.

1.
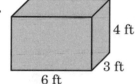
6 ft   4 ft   3 ft

2.
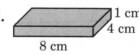
1 cm   4 cm   8 cm

3.
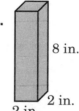
8 in.   2 in.   2 in.

4.
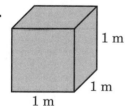
1 m   1 m   1 m

5.
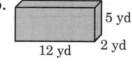
5 yd   12 yd   2 yd

6.
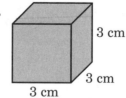
3 cm   3 cm   3 cm

Apply the Idea

7. Suppose you want to wrap a gift box that measures 24 inches by 14 inches by 10 inches. Can you wrap the box in a piece of paper that is 24 inches by 48 inches? Explain why or why not.

Write About It

8. Based on how you found the surface area of a rectangular prism, explain how you would find the surface area of a triangular prism.

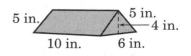
5 in.   5 in.   4 in.   10 in.   6 in.

⬇️ **7.8** Finding Volume

In This lesson, You Will Learn
To find the volume of three-dimensional figures

Words to Learn
Volume the amount of space enclosed by a three-dimensional figure

Cube a rectangular prism with square sides

Cubic units volume is measured in cubic units, such as cubic feet, cubic yards, and cubic meters

Cylinder a three-dimensional figure with a pair of parallel circular bases of the same size connected by a curved surface

---

This storage locker is 5 feet long, 3 feet wide, and 4 feet high. How much storage space is in the locker?

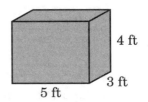

New Idea
The measure of the space inside a three-dimensional shape is called the **volume**. Think of volume as the number of cubes needed to fill a three-dimensional figure.

The rectangular prism below is filled with cubes that measure 1 foot on every side. Each cube is 1 cubic foot, or 1 ft^3. You can count 60 cubes, so the volume of the rectangular prism is 60 cubic feet or 60 ft^3. We call this kind of measurement **cubic units**.

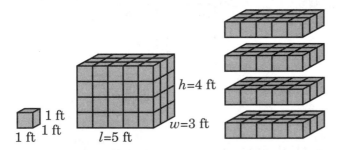

You can also find the volume of a rectangular prism by multiplying its three dimensions. Use the formula: Volume = length × width × height.

$V = l \times w \times h$

$V = 5 \times 3 \times 4$ Replace *l*, *w*, and *h* with the locker's dimensions.

$V = 60$

The volume of the storage locker is 60 cubic feet or 60 ft^3.
You can use the same formula, $V = l \times w \times h$, to find the volume of a **cube**, a rectangular prism with square sides.

To find the volume of a **cylinder**, first find the area of the circular base (the area of a circle $= \pi \times r^2$) and multiply it by the height.

Volume of a cylinder $= \pi \times r^2 \times h$

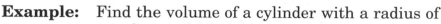

r = 3 in.

h = 6 in.

Example: Find the volume of a cylinder with a radius of 3 inches and a height of 6 inches.

Step 1: Write the formula for volume of a cylinder. $V = \pi \times r^2 \times h$

Step 2: Replace π with 3.14, r with 3 inches, and h with 6 inches.
$V = \pi \times r \times r \times h$
$V \approx 3.14 \times 3 \times 3 \times 6$

Step 3: Multiply to find the volume. $V \approx 169.56$

The volume of the cylinder is about 169.56 in³.

Focus on the Idea

To find the volume of a rectangular prism, multiply length x width x height.
$$V = l \times w \times h$$
To find the volume of a cylinder, multiply the base area of the circle $(\pi \times r^2)$ by the height.
$$V = \pi \times r^2$$

Practice *Show your work on a separate sheet of paper.*

 Find the volume of each figure. You may wish to use a calculator. Round any decimals to the nearest hundredth. Use 3.14 for π.

1.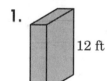
12 ft
7 ft
3 ft

2. 10 m
10 m
10 m

3.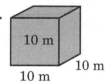
4 cm
16 cm

4.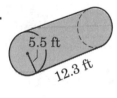
5.5 ft
12.3 ft

5. Prism
   length = 5 inches
   width = 4 inches
   height = 7 inches

6. Cube
   edge = 4 centimeters

7. Cylinder
   radius = 6 yards
   height = 9 yards

 Apply the Idea

8. A gardener is planting a small tree in a large cylindrical planter. She needs one bag of potting soil for every cubic foot of planter. If the radius of the planter is 2 feet and its height is 3 feet, how many whole bags of potting soil does she need?

Write About It

9. Why is the formula for the volume of a cylinder different from the one for rectangular prisms? How are the two formulas the same? Explain.

 **Chapter 7** Review

In This Chapter, You Have Learned

- To identify various polygons
- To find the perimeter of polygons
- To find the area of rectangles, squares, and other parallelograms
- To find the area of triangles
- To find the circumference of circles
- To find the area of circles
- To find the area of irregular figures
- To find the surface area of three-dimensional figures
- To find the volume of three-dimensional figures

Words You Know

From the lists of Words to Learn, choose the word or phrase that best completes each statement.

1. The distance around a circle is called the ___.

2. A ___ is a rectangle with 4 equal sides.

3. An object that has length, width, and height is called ___.

4. The line that passes through the center of the circle with both ends on the circle is the ___.

5. The ___ of a three-dimensional figure is a measure of the amount of space it encloses.

6. The distance around a polygon is called the ___.

7. ___ is the amount of surface a figure covers.

More Practice *Show your work on a separate sheet of paper.*

Write the formula for the area of each figure.

8. parallelogram

9. triangle

10. circle

Find the perimeter and area of each figure.

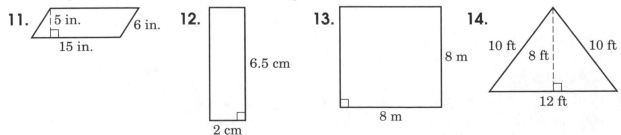

11. 5 in. / 6 in. / 15 in.

12. 6.5 cm / 2 cm

13. 8 m / 8 m

14. 10 ft / 8 ft / 10 ft / 12 ft

15.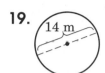
11 m 8 m 4 m 9 m

16.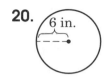
1.5 cm 1.5 cm

17.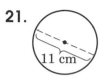
8.5 km 3.3 km 7.8 km

18.
6 yd 7.1 yd 8.5 yd

Find the circumference and area of each circle.

19.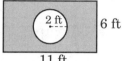
14 m

20.
6 in.

21.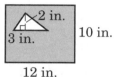
11 cm

22.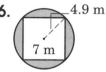
3.5 ft

Find the area of the shaded region of each figure.

23.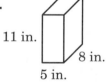
2 ft 6 ft 11 ft

24.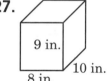
5 cm 5 cm 8 cm

25.
2 in. 3 in. 10 in. 12 in.

26.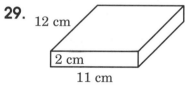
4.9 m 7 m

Find the surface area of each figure.

27.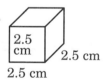
9 in. 10 in. 8 in.

28.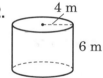
10 ft 10 ft 10 ft

29.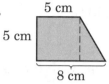
12 cm 2 cm 11 cm

Find the volume of each figure.

30.
11 in. 8 in. 5 in.

31.
2.5 cm 2.5 cm 2.5 cm

32.
4 m 6 m

Problems You Can Solve

Use the diagram to the right to answer the questions.

Friendship Park
Playing Field Picnic Space 1 km 2 km
8 km 7 km 1.5 km 1.5 km
4 km 5 km Hiking Trails Boating Lake
3 km 9 km

33. Find the area of the Picnic Space.

34. Which has the greater area: the Playing Field or the Boating Lake?

35. How much of the park do the Hiking Trails take up?

36. There is a running track around the Boating Lake. What is the distance around the lake?

37. The whole park is covered in a special turf, except for the Playing Field, the Picnic Space, the Hiking Trails, and the Boating Lake. How much area does the turf cover?

Chapter 7 Practice Test

Find the perimeter and area of each figure.

1.
6.2 cm
12.5 cm

2.
2.1 ft
2.1 ft

3.
11 in. 5 in.
2 in.
8 in.

4.
6 yd 7.1 yd
8.5 yd

Find the area of each figure with these dimensions.

5. rectangle
base = 40 centimeters
height =12 centimeters

6. square
side = 1.4 meters

7. triangle
base = 9 yards
height = 8.6 yards

Find the circumference and area of each circle with these dimensions. Use 3.14 for π.

8. diameter = 12 inches

9. radius = 25 millimeters

10. radius = 5 feet

Find the area of the shaded region.

11.
12 in.
15 in.
6 in.
20 in.

12.
24 km
4 km
8 km
13 km

Find the surface area of each figure with these dimensions.

13. rectangular prism
length = 12 feet
width = 5 feet
height = 6 feet

14. cube
edge = 8 inches

Find the volume of each figure with these dimensions. Use 3.14 for π.

15. rectangular prism
length = 30 meters
width = 14 meters
height = 8 meters

16. cube
edge = 6 inches

17. cylinder
diameter = 6 feet
height = 18 feet

Solve.

18. Marcel wants to rent a storage locker that measures 12 feet by 12 feet by 8 feet. What is the volume of the storage locker?

19. Luiz is preparing a circular outdoor skating rink that has a diameter of 50 meters. What is the area of the skating rink?

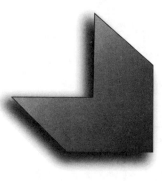

Chapter 8
Statistics

In this chapter, you will learn

- To find the mean, median, and mode of data
- To organize information in frequency tables
- To read and make bar graphs
- To read and make line graphs
- To read circle graphs
- To identify statistics that are misleading

The media we read, watch, and listen to use statistics all the time. TV news, newspapers, and magazines use statistics to report on sports, policy, weather, and consumer information. Showing statistics in tables and graphs helps people better understand information. For example, you could use the graph below to answer questions like these:

What is the mean number of cars per 1,000 inhabitants for the countries shown on the graph? What is the median number of cars per 1,000 inhabitants? About how many cars per 1,000 inhabitants are there in the country with the most cars?

In this chapter you will learn how to find and use some statistical measures called mean, mode, and median. You will learn how to use data to make graphs to help you communicate information and how to read graphs to find information.

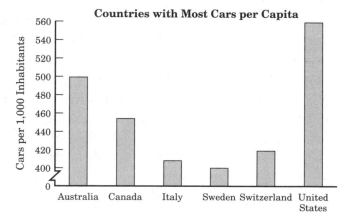

Countries with Most Cars per Capita

8.1 Finding the Mean, Median, and Mode

In This Lesson, You Will Learn

To find the mean, median, and mode of data

Words to Learn

Data information gathered, usually in the form of numbers

Statistics the study of data

Mean the sum of the data divided by the number of pieces of data

Median the middle number when data are ordered from least to greatest

Mode the number that appears most often in a set of data

Joe and his father are trying to decide how many apples to stock in their market. To help make a decision, Joe asks 11 people leaving the market how many apples they buy each week. He gathers the following information.

7, 5, 6, 1, 5, 3, 5, 1, 25, 6, 2

How can Joe talk about these numbers without listing them all?

New Idea

The numbers Joe collected are called **data** because they provide information about something—in this case, the number of apples people buy in a week. The study of data is called **statistics.**

One way Joe can talk about or represent the whole set of data with one number is to find the **mean** of the data. The mean is sometimes called the average. The mean should always be a number that falls between the smallest piece of data and the largest piece of data. To find the mean, add the data and divide the sum by the number of pieces of data.

mean = sum ÷ number of pieces of data

mean = $(7 + 5 + 6 + 1 + 5 + 3 + 5 + 1 + 25 + 6 + 2) \div 11$

mean = $(66) \div 11 = 6$

The mean number of apples people buy in a week is 6.

The mean is not always a whole number.

Example: Find the mean number of children in 6 families with
1, 3, 1, 6, 4, and 2 children.

Step 1: Add the data. $\qquad\qquad$ $1 + 3 + 1 + 6 + 4 + 2 = 17$

Step 2: Divide the sum by the number of $\qquad$ $17 \div 6 = 2.83333$
pieces of data (6).

The mean number of children is about 2.8.

The number 0 counts like any other piece of data.

Example: Find the mean of 78, 90, 88, 91, and 0.

Step 1: Add the numbers. $\qquad\qquad$ $78 + 90 + 88 + 91 + 0 = 347$

Step 2: Divide the sum by the number of $\qquad$ $347 \div 5 = 69.4$
pieces of data (5).

The mean of the numbers is 69.4.

✓ Check the Math

An article listed the monthly rainfall in inches over a 6-month
period as 1, 3, 3, 5, 3, 4. The article then said the mean rainfall was
5.2 inches. Could this be the mean? How do you know?

Focus on the Idea

To find the mean of a set of data, add the data and divide the sum
by the number of pieces of data.

Practice *Show your work on a separate sheet of paper.*
Find the mean of each set of data

1. 7, 12, 15, 22, 8 $\qquad\qquad$ 2. 370, 400, 229, 388

3. 75, 82, 90, 100 $\qquad\qquad$ 4. 75, 82, 90, 0, 100

5. .26, 1.10, 2.52, 2.05, 3, .72 $\quad$ 6. $1\frac{1}{2}$, 3, $\frac{1}{4}$, $1\frac{1}{8}$, $2\frac{1}{8}$

Extend the Idea

The middle number in a set of data that is ordered from least to
greatest is called the **median**. Like the mean, this number can also
be used to represent a set of data.

Be careful when you reorder the numbers from least to greatest.
First count the list, then make sure each piece of data matches the
original list.

Example: Find the median of 7, 5, 6, 1, 5, 3, 5, 1, 25, 6, and 2.

    Step 1: Order the numbers from least to greatest.   1, 1, 2, 3, 5, 5, 5, 6, 6, 7, 25

    Step 2: Find the middle number.   1, 1, 2, 3, 5, <u>5</u>, 5, 6, 6, 7, 25

           The median of the set of numbers is 5.

Sometimes the median is not in the set of data; if the number of pieces of data is even, there is no middle number. To find the median of an even number of data, pick out the 2 middle numbers and find their mean.

Example: Find the median of 16, 12, 20, 13, 17, and 20.

    Step 1: Order the numbers from least to greatest.   12, 13, 16, 17, 20, 20

    Step 2: Find the 2 middle numbers.   12, 13, <u>16, 17</u>, 20, 20

    Step 3: Find the mean of the two middle numbers. $(16 + 17) \div 2 = 16.5$

           The median of the set of data is 16.5.

You can also represent a set of data with the number that appears the most often. This number is called the **mode**. It is easier to find the mode when the numbers are ordered from least to greatest.

Example: Find the mode of 7, 5, 6, 1, 5, 3, 5, 1, 25, 6, and 2.

    Order the numbers.   1, 1, 2, 3, 5, 5, 5, 6, 6, 7, 25

    The number 5 appears the most often.
    5 is the mode.

There can be more than one mode or no mode.

Example 1: Find the mode of 98, 102, 101, 98, 96, and 102.

    Order the numbers.   96, 98, 98, 101, 102, 102

    Both 98 and 102 appear twice.
    The modes are 98 and 102.

Example 2: Find the mode of 12, 25, 13, 16, 17, and 22.

    Order the numbers.   12, 13, 16, 17, 22, 25

    All the numbers appear the same number of times (once). There is no mode.

✓ Check Your Understanding

Look at the data below.

    12, 12, 12, 14, 14, 17, 20, 29, 30

Without doing any calculations, try to tell which of the numbers below is the mean. Which is the median? Which is the mode? Which do you think best represents the data?

    a. 14   **b.** 12   **c.** 17.8

 Practice *Show your work on a separate sheet of paper.*

Find the median and mode of each set of data.

7. 25, 4, 70, 33, 22

8. 100, 350, 220, 280, 190

9. 25, 37, 39, 35, 25, 19, 23, 25, 19

10. 87, 66, 78, 92, 45, 74, 56, 49, 80, 75, 93, 81

11. 251, 372, 118, 354, 372, 265, 265, 241, 272, 265

12. 346, 120, 248, 183, 120, 185, 248, 120, 248, 190

Find the mean of each set of data.

13. 28, 35, 21, 20   **14.** 64, 57, 82, 69

15. 12, 38, 41, 7, 56   **16.** 50, 31, 14, 79, 79, 52

17. 2, 4, 6, 8, 10, 12, 14   **18.** 15.5, 10, 8.1, 24, 17

Apply the Idea

19. Francesca scored in each of the last 7 basketball games she played. These are her scores: 12, 6, 2, 16, 12, 20, 12.

    a. What is her mean score?

    b. What is her median score?

    c. What is the mode of her scores?

20. Find the mean, the mode, and the median of these daytime high temperatures for one week.

    67°   72°   68°   70°   67°   73°   66°

Write About It

21. Find the mean and median of the following set of data. Which number better represents the data. Why?

    2, 3, 2, 0, 1, 22

In This Lesson, You Will Learn

To organize information in frequency tables

Words to Learn

Frequency table a chart that shows how often a number or item appears in a set of data

Score a piece of data

Minimum the smallest number in a set of data

Maximum the largest number in a set of data

An athletic footwear company wants to survey people to find out how many pairs of sneakers they own. A researcher interviews 35 people to ask how many pairs of sneakers they have in their closets. He gives his boss the following list:

4, 2, 3, 5, 1, 4, 2, 1, 2, 3, 1, 4, 7, 5, 3, 6, 1, 0, 1, 5, 4, 4, 3, 5, 2, 4, 6, 2, 9, 3, 4, 2, 2, 3, 4

His boss tells him to organize the numbers so that they are easier to read and give more information about the survey results.

New Idea

The researcher can reorganize the information into a **frequency table** to show how often a number occurs in the data. A frequency table has two columns. The first shows the numbers, or **scores**, that make up the data and the second shows the frequency of each score.

To make a frequency table, you must first find the smallest score in the data, the **minimum**, and the largest score, the **maximum**. The first column of the table must show all the possible scores between the minimum and the maximum, even if they do not appear in the data. In the second column, record how often each of the scores appears in the set of data. You may find it helpful to use tally marks to keep track of how often each score appears as you go through the list of data.

When you finish the table, add the numbers in the frequency column. The sum should equal the number of scores.

You can quickly answer many questions or find many pieces of information when data is organized in a frequency table.

	Pairs of Sneakers Owned	Frequency
I	0	1
JHT	1	5
JHT II	2	7
JHT I	3	6
JHT III	4	8
IIII	5	4
II	6	2
I	7	1
	8	0
I	9	1
	Total:	35

Example 1: Find the number of people surveyed who own 5 pairs of sneakers.

Find 5 under "Pairs of Sneakers Owned" and read across to the Frequency column.

4 people own 5 pairs of sneakers.

Example 2: Find the number of people surveyed who own fewer than 4 pairs of sneakers.

Look in the Frequency column to find the numbers of people who own 3, 2, 1, and 0 pairs. Add the numbers.

$6 + 7 + 5 + 1 = 19$

19 of the people surveyed own fewer than 4 pairs of sneakers.

✓ Check Your Understanding

Explain what is wrong with the first column of this frequency table of test scores for 20 students.

Test Scores	Frequency
90	1
92	2
95	4
96	3
100	10

Focus on the Idea

A frequency table organizes data to show how many times each score occurs in a set of data. The table must show all the possible scores between the minimum and maximum scores of the data.

Practice   *Show your work on a separate sheet of paper.*

1. Make a frequency table for the number of books read in one month by 25 students.

    5, 3, 5, 3, 1, 8, 2, 4, 3, 5, 9, 6, 7, 8, 8, 10, 2, 5, 3, 4, 5, 3, 3, 5, 2

2. Make a frequency table for the price of a movie at 15 different movie theaters.

    $7, $7.50, $7, $8, $6, $6.50, $7, $8, $8, $8.50, $7.50, $7, $8, $6.50, $6.50

    a. How many movie theaters charge $6.50?

    b. How many movie theaters charge more than $7.50?

3. Use the frequency table of quiz scores to answer the questions.

Quiz Scores	Frequency
4	1
5	4
6	4
7	6
8	7
9	1

a. How many students scored an 8?

b. How many students scored 5 or more?

c. How many students took the quiz?

Extend the Idea

You can use a frequency table to find the mean, median, and mode.

Student headcount in homeroom classes	
Students	**Frequency**
25	1
26	2
27	2
28	2
29	4

To find the mean you first must find the sum of the data. It is easier to find the sum of the data for each row in the table, then add the sums of the rows. For example, the frequency table shows that 4 classes have 29 students. You have to add 29 four times. A shortcut is to multiply 29 by 4, or multiply each score by its frequency. Once you have multiplied across each row, add the products and divide by the total number of pieces of data.

Example: Find the mean number of students per class in the 11 classes.

Step 1: Multiply scores by frequencies.

Step 2: Add the products to find the sum.

Students	Frequency	Students × Frequency
25	1	25 × 1 = 25
26	2	26 × 2 = 52
27	2	27 × 2 = 54
28	2	28 × 2 = 56
29	4	29 × 4 = 116

number of classes = 11   sum = 303

Step 3: Divide the sum by the number of pieces of data (11).

$$303 \div 11 = 27.5454$$

The mean number of students in a class is about 27.5.

To find the median you could write out all the scores and then find the middle number.

25, 26, 26, 27, 27, <u>28</u>, 28, 29, 29, 29, 29

You can also use a frequency table and the total number of scores to find the median. Divide the total number of scores by 2. The quotient tells which score is the middle score. If the total number of classes is an odd number, you will get a decimal quotient that you must round up to the nearest whole number. Then, add the frequencies from either the top or bottom to locate the middle score.

Example 1: Find the median number of students per class in the 11 classes.

Step 1: Divide the total number of scores by 2.　　$11 \div 2 = 5.5$

Step 2: If the quotient is a decimal, round it up.　　$5.5 \rightarrow 6$

Step 3: To find the median score, add the frequencies until you get to the quotient 6 or the first number over the quotient.

The median number of students is 28.

Students	Frequency	
25	1	
26	2	$2 + 1 = 3$
27	2	$2 + 3 = 5$
28	2	$2 + 5 = \text{⑦}$
29	4	$4 + 7 = 11$

7 is the first number greater than 6.

If the total number of scores is even, the median will be the average of the two middle scores. For the quiz scores of 18 students divide $18 \div 2 = 9$. The median is between the 9th and 10th scores.

$5, 5, 5, 5, 5, 6, 6, 6, \underline{6, 7}, 7, 7, 8, 8, 8, 8, 8, 8$

The median is $(6 + 7) \div 2 = 6.5$.

You also can add the frequencies in the table to find the middle two scores.

Scores	Frequency
5	5
6	4
7	3
8	6

9　12

To find the mode, find the score with the highest frequency.

Example: Find the mode of the quiz scores for the 18 students.

6 is the highest frequency, so 8 is the mode.

Practice *Show your work on a separate sheet of paper.*

4. Find the mean, median, and mode of the data in the table at the right.

Age of Part-Time Employees at Video Store	
Age	**Frequency**
16	1
17	2
18	0
19	1
20	3
21	2

Apply the Idea

5. Kelleher Realty Corp. wants to put up a new building. The town zoning laws say that the height of any new building cannot exceed the mean or median (whichever is greater) of the building heights on the block. Make a frequency table with the heights of the other buildings on the block where Kelleher Realty wants to put its new building:

   26 ft, 30 ft, 28 ft, 22 ft, 22 ft, 26 ft, 27 ft, 31 ft, 24 ft

   How tall a building is Kelleher Realty allowed to build?

Write About It

6. Explain the steps you would take to make a frequency table for the life span in years of 9 cars.

   5, 2, 5, 6, 7, 8, 4, 9, 7

8.3 Reading and Making Bar Graphs

In This Lesson, You Will Learn

To read and to make bar graphs

Words to Learn

Bar graph a graph that uses bars to show a set of data that can be separated into distinct groups

Vertical axis the line up the side of the graph

Scale a series of marks that measure equal distances on a line

Horizontal axis the line along the bottom of the graph

While researching for a report on the Olympics, Molly found the graph below of data on the number of countries that participated in the last 6 summer Olympics. How can she read the graph to find information for her report?

New Idea

This graph is called a **bar graph** because it uses bars to show data. You can use bar graphs to organize information and to compare amounts. The title tells what the graph is about.

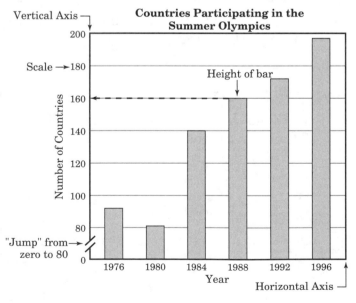

The **vertical axis** shows the number of countries. The **scale** measures equal distances along the vertical axis. The spaces between the marks are called intervals. In this graph each interval stands for 20 countries. The scale must always start at zero and include the maximum number in the data. Sometimes a jump in numbers in the first interval is shown as a break in the scale.

The **horizontal axis** shows the years being compared. All bars are the same width and there is the same amount of space between each bar. The height of each bar shows the number of countries for that year.

You can use a bar graph to find information and answer questions quickly.

Example 1: Did the number of countries increase every year?

Look to see whether the bars always increase in height from left to right.

No, the numbers did not increase every year; they dropped in 1980.

Example 2: Find the number of countries that participated in 1992.

Find the bar for 1992 and look across from the top of the bar to the scale.

The top of 1992 is a little more than 170, or around 172.

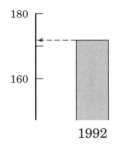

Example 3: Between which 2 consecutive Olympics was there the biggest change?

Find the two bars next to each other with the largest height difference.

The biggest change was between 1980 and 1984.

Focus on the Idea

You can use a bar graph to display data and compare amounts.

Practice *Show your work on a separate sheet of paper.*

Use the bar graph to answer the questions.

1. Which country won the fewest medals?

2. Which won the most medals?

3. About how many more medals did China win than France?

4. Germany won about how many more medals than Russia?

5. Write the countries in order from least to most medals won.

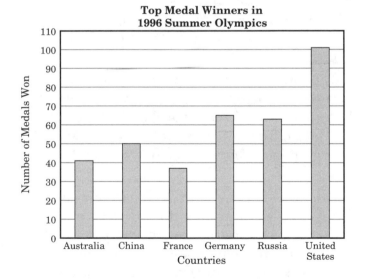

Apply the Idea

6. In the 1996 Summer Olympics, Russian athletes won 26 gold medals, 21 silver medals, and 16 bronze medals. Make a bar graph that displays this data. Be sure to label each axis clearly and include a scale.

Write About It

7. Write one more question about the graph shown for Problems 1–5.

8.4 Reading and Making Line Graphs

In This Lesson, You Will Learn

To read and to make line graphs

Words to Learn

Line graph a graph that is used to show continuous change over time

Trend pattern of change over time

Ronnie's bank sent him a graph to show how much money he had in his savings account at the end of each month over 7 months. How can Ronnie use the graph to get a better idea of his savings habits?

New Ideas

Ronnie's graph is a **line graph**. A line graph shows continuous data that change over time but are recorded only at specific times. The graph shows what Ronnie's savings were at the end of each month.

Line graphs are often used to show **trends** or patterns of change over time. The steepness of the lines shows how fast the data change. A very steep line shows fast change. A flatter line shows slow change.

The scale of the vertical axis includes the minimum and maximum scores or pieces of data and is broken into even intervals. The scale does not have to start at zero. The horizontal axis shows the time in even intervals over which the data was recorded.

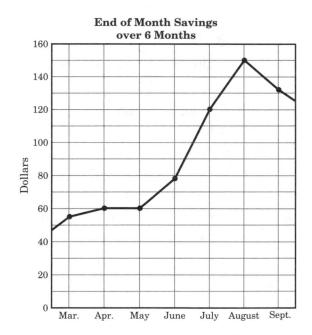

To read the graph, look at each point on the graph in relation to its dollar value (shown on the scale on the vertical axis) and the specific time (on the horizontal axis). The steepness of the lines that connect the points also provides information.

Example 1: Find the amount of money Ronnie had in savings at the end of March.

Locate March on the vertical axis. Find the point above March on the graph and follow it across to the scale.

Ronnie had about $56 in savings at the end of March.

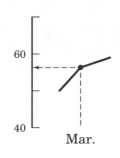

Example 2: Find the month in which Ronnie's savings did not change.

The line between April and May is flat. There was no change in Ronnie's savings from April to May.

Example 3: What trend do the summer months show?

Between June, July, and August, the lines have the steepest increase. Ronnie saved the most in the summer.

Focus on the Idea

Line graphs show continuous change over time and often help to identify trends.

Practice *Show your work on a separate sheet of paper.*

Use the line graph to answer Problems 1–3.

1. What was the average number of rentals in a week in 1985?

2. In which years were the most videos rented per week?

3. What is the trend in video rentals between 1983 and 1991?

4. What do you think will happen after 1995?

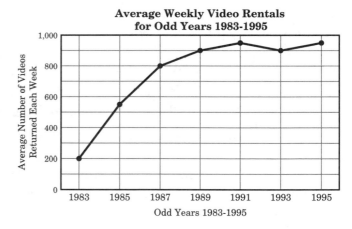

Apply the Idea

5. Draw a line graph to show the data given here from the share price of a stock over 8 days. Make the scale start at $15, end at $18.50, and increase in $.25 intervals.

Day	Price	Day	Price
1	$16	5	$18
2	$15.75	6	$17.75
3	$16	7	$17
4	$16.75	8	$17.50

Write About It

6. Use the graph of Ronnie's savings to explain why you think his savings increased and dropped off when they did.

8.5 Reading Circle Graphs

In This Lesson, You Will Learn
To read circle graphs

Words to Learn
Circle graph a graph that is used to show the relationship of parts of a set of data to the whole set of data

A sporting goods store sells $5,000 worth of sports equipment in a single weekend. The store manager has to send her sales figures to headquarters. She makes a circle graph that shows how much was sold in each sports category.

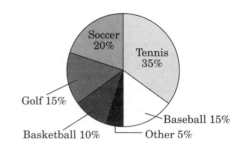

New Idea

A **circle graph** shows how one part of the data compares to the whole. The whole circle represents the total. The parts are usually represented as percents of the whole. The sum of all parts is always 100%.

Example: Find what percent of total sales is basketball equipment.

The part labeled *basketball* says 10%.

Basketball equipment is 10% of total sales.

When you have a number that represents the whole, you can use percents to find the actual amount in each part. Multiply the percent by the whole.

Example: Find the actual sales of baseball equipment.

Step 1:   Find the percent.   15%

Step 2:   Write the percent as a decimal.   15% = .15

Step 3:   Multiply by the whole.   .15 × 5,000 = 750

$750 in baseball equipment was sold.

You can use a circle graph without numbers to compare and estimate amounts. The graph on the top of page 141 shows how Gen spends her budget of $2,000 a month.

Example 1: Estimate how much Gen spends on rent.

The section labeled *Rent* takes up a little less than half of the circle.

Half of $2,000 is $1,000.

Gen spends a little less than $1,000 on rent.

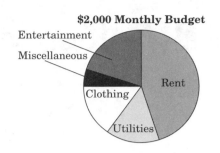

$2,000 Monthly Budget

Example 2: Find the 2 items on which Gen spends about the same amount.

The sections labeled *Utilities* and *Clothing* are about the same size.

Gen spends about the same amount on utilities and clothing.

Focus on the Idea

Circle graphs show the relationship of pieces of data to the whole and to each other.

Practice *Show your work on a separate sheet of paper.*

A sporting goods store sold $750,000 of apparel and footwear. This circle graph represents how much was sold in each category. Use it to answer Problems 1–5.

1. What percent of the total sales was in shirts?

2. Which product was the smallest part of total sales?

3. What were dollar sales of shoes?

4. What were dollar sales of hats?

5. What were dollar sales of shorts?

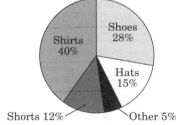

Apply the Idea

A magazine asked its readers to vote on their favorite of 5 books. The magazine printed the results as a circle graph. Use the graph to answer Problems 6–8.

6. Which book received about $\frac{1}{4}$ of the votes?

7. Which two books received about the same number of votes?

8. If 2,500 people voted, about how many voted for book B?

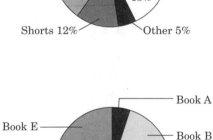

Write About It

9. Explain what is wrong with this circle graph. How could you correct it?

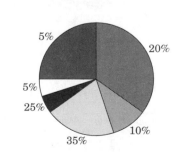

In This Lesson, You Will Learn
To identify statistics that are misleading

In a magazine article about a tropical city, Luis read that the city's average monthly rainfall last year was 15.3 inches. When Luis checked further, he found that although the average rainfall was indeed 15.3 inches, the median rainfall was 1 inch and the mode was 0 inches. The table shows the actual monthly rainfall.

Month	Rainfall (in inches)
January	0
February	0
March	0
April	0
May	2
June	53
July	69
August	41
September	30
October	5
November	0
December	0

New Idea

Statistics can be misleading. Graphs, polls or surveys, and averages can be misunderstood depending on the way statistics are presented. Based on the average monthly rainfall statistic in the article, Luis might easily assume that some rain fell every month of the year.

A bar graph is a better way than the table to present the data because it shows the entire picture of the rainfall. You can see that nearly all the rain fell in just four months: June, July, August, and September.

The magazine article did not give any incorrect information, but by failing to give important information, it could easily leave the reader with the wrong impression of the city's climate.

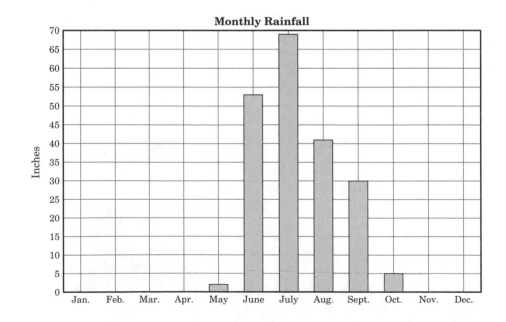

Another way to create a misleading impression is to manipulate the scale on a line or bar graph. Big jumps in scale or uneven intervals can exaggerate trends.

Example: Explain how this graph makes the increase in quarterly sales appear so great. Find the actual increase in sales between the first and second quarters.

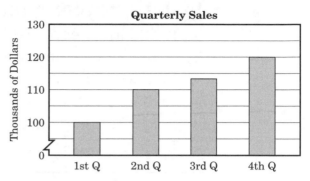

By jumping the vertical scale from 0 to 100, the graph gives the impression that second quarter sales were double first quarter sales. In fact, sales were $100,000 in the first quarter and $110,000 in the second—a difference of only $10,000.

Focus on the Idea

When graphs or statistics are misused, they give the wrong impression. You must carefully analyze graphs and statistics to determine whether they are being properly presented.

Practice *Show your work on a separate sheet of paper.*

Use the line graph to answer Problems 1–3.

1. How many degrees difference is there between the coolest and the warmest hourly daytime temperatures?

2. How big was the drop in temperature from 11 A.M. to noon? Do you think the change in temperature would be noticeable?

3. What could you do to the scale to make the changes in temperature appear even more dramatic?

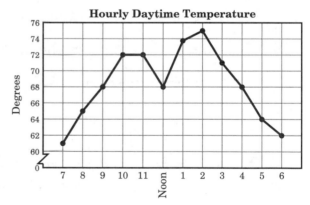

Apply the Idea

Use the table of data on math scores to answer Problems 4 and 5.

4. Draw a bar graph without a jump in the vertical axis to show a small change in math scores over the 6 grading periods.

5. Redraw the bar graph with a jump in the vertical axis that exaggerates the drop in the math scores.

Grading Period	Average Math Score
1	85
2	83
3	80
4	79
5	75
6	72

Write About It

6. Find a graph in a magazine or newspaper. Write about how well you think the graph represents the data.

Chapter 8 Review

In this chapter, you have learned

- To find the mean, median, and mode of data
- To organize information in frequency tables
- To read and make bar graphs
- To read and make line graphs
- To read circle graphs
- To identify statistics that are misleading

Words You Know

From the lists of Words to Learn, choose the word or phrase that completes each statement.

1. A pattern change over time is called a ___.

2. The ___ is the middle number in a set of data ordered from least to greatest.

3. The smallest number in a set of data is the ___.

4. A ___ is a graph that shows change over time.

5. Information gathered in the form of numbers is called ___.

6. The number that appears the most often in a set of data is the ___.

7. A ___ is a chart used to show how often a number or item appears in a set of data.

More Practice *Show your work on a separate sheet of paper.*

Find the mean, median, and mode for each set of data.

8. 30, 33, 21, 45, 46

9. 12, 8, 0, 3, 15, 18, 12

10. 1, 1, 0, 3, 1, 1, 2, 3

11. .5, .6, 3, .10, .04, .1

12. $\frac{1}{2}, \frac{3}{4}, \frac{1}{8}, \frac{3}{4}, \frac{3}{4}, \frac{3}{8}, \frac{1}{4}$

13. 12, 35, 35, 43, 12, 98, 15

14. 27 people were asked how many televisions they have in their homes. The results are shown below.

6	3	4	2	3	5	3	7	1
3	4	3	3	4	3	9	3	2
6	1	3	5	3	2	4	3	9

a. Make a frequency table for the data.
b. Find the mean of the data.
c. Find the mode of the data.

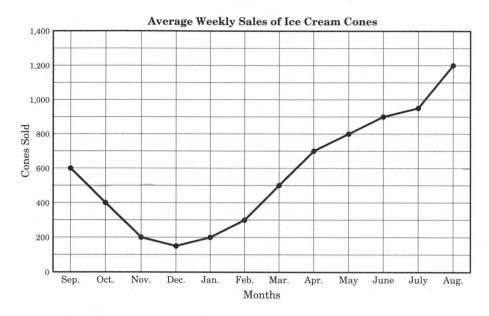

Average Weekly Sales of Ice Cream Cones

Cones Sold (y-axis: 0, 200, 400, 600, 800, 1,000, 1,200, 1,400)

Months (x-axis: Sep., Oct., Nov., Dec., Jan., Feb., Mar., Apr., May, June, July, Aug.)

15. The line graph above shows the weekly average number of ice cream cones sold by one store over a 12-month period.

  a. On average, about how many ice cream cones were sold each week in June?

  b. On average, about how many ice cream cones were sold each week in January?

  c. Between which 2 months was there the largest increase in ice cream cone sales?

  d. What would you expect to happen to sales next September?

16. The circle graph shows how the money from the sale of a $15 CD is distributed.

  a. What percent of the money is for manufacturing?

  b. How much money is for the artists?

  c. How much money is for profit?

  d. Which category gets about one-third of the money?

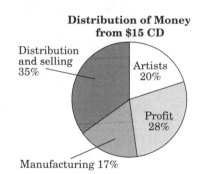

Distribution of Money from $15 CD

Distribution and selling 35%
Artists 20%
Profit 28%
Manufacturing 17%

Problems You Can Solve

Use the bar graph to answer Problems 17–20.

17. What is the mean number of cars per 1,000 inhabitants for the countries shown on the graph?

18. What is the median number of cars per 1,000 inhabitants?

19. How many cars per 1,000 inhabitants are there in the country with the fewest cars?

20. About how many cars per 1,000 inhabitants are there in the country with the most cars?

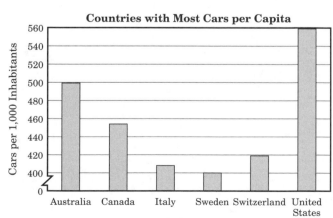

Countries with Most Cars per Capita

Cars per 1,000 Inhabitants (y-axis: 0, 400, 420, 440, 460, 480, 500, 520, 540, 560)

(x-axis: Australia, Canada, Italy, Sweden, Switzerland, United States)

Find the mean, median, and mode for each set of data.

1. 12, 16, 13, 11, 13

2. 25, 33, 46, 28, 10, 50

3. 3, 4, 5, 1, 1, 6, 1, 29, 4

4. In Problem 3, does the median or mean better represent the data?

Use the graphs and tables to answer the questions.

5. Use this frequency table of scores on a 10-point quiz to answer the following questions.

   a. How many students took the quiz?

   b. How many students scored a 9?

   c. How many students scored less than 6?

   d. What was the mean score?

Score	Frequency
4	2
5	3
6	2
7	5
8	0
9	1

6. The circle graph shows the $25,000 school budget for computer equipment and supplies.

   a. How much is spent for printers?

   b. On which item is the least amount spent?

   c. How does the amount spent on scanners compare to the amount spent on software?

   d. What percent is spent on scanners?

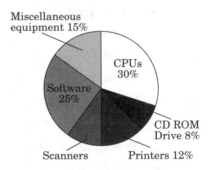

7. The chart at right shows the temperature in degrees Fahrenheit at midnight for one week.

   a. Make a line graph to show the data.

   b. What trend does the graph show?

Temperature at Midnight (F°)

Su.	M.	Tu.	W.	Th.	F.	Sat.
59	61	55	53	50	50	48

8. The circle graph at right shows the graduation rates for 6 cities, labeled A, B, C, D, E, and F.

   a. Why is a circle graph not appropriate for this data?

   b. What kind of graph would better show the graduation rates?

Percent of Students Who Graduate After 4 Years of H.S.

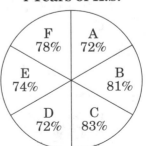

Chapter 9
Probability

In this chapter, you will learn

- To find the sample space of a game
- To decide whether a game is fair
- To find the probability of an event
- To make a tree diagram
- To read a tree diagram to list possible outcomes
- To find the number of possible outcomes by multiplying
- To find the probability of two or more events

At the start of a football game, a coin is tossed to determine which team will receive the ball first. This is a fair way to start a game because there is an equally likely chance that the coin will come up heads or tails. But there are often more than 2 possible outcomes in an event. A combination of choices or possibilities results in many possible outcomes.

Look at the objects to the right. Think of all the possible games or activities you could create with these objects. What is the chance, probability, that you pick a red marble from the jar? What are all the possible outcomes if you toss the coin and then pick a marble? How many possible outcomes are there if you pick a marble and then pick a letter?

In this chapter you will learn to use diagrams and multiplication to determine the probability of a specific event, such as spinning a number, drawing a special card, or winning the lottery.

9.1 Finding Outcomes of Games

In This Lesson, You Will Learn

To find the sample space of a game

To decide whether a game is fair

Words to Learn

At random a condition in which outcomes happen without influence

Outcome the result of an activity, experiment, or game

Sample space the list of all possible outcomes of an activity

Event specific outcome or outcomes

Fair game a game in which each player has an equal chance of winning

Joe and Laura will use this spinner to decide who gets to use their bicycle today. Laura gets the bike if the spinner lands on an odd number. Joe gets the bike if it lands on an even number. Is this game fair?

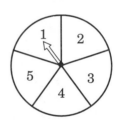

New Idea

The spinner will land on a number **at random**, which means that neither person is influencing the spin. To decide whether the game is fair, you need to list all the possible **outcomes**, or the possible results of spinning the spinner. This list is called the **sample space**. The sample space for this spinner is 1, 2, 3, 4, 5.

Each outcome is equally likely because all of the numbered sections of the spinner are the same size. But Joe and Laura each want a different **event,** or specific outcome. Joe wants the event of landing on an even number: 2 or 4. Laura wants the event of landing on an odd number: 1, 3, or 5.

Because there are more outcomes in Laura's event, she has a better chance of winning. The game is not fair. In a **fair game**, all players have an equal chance of winning.

Example: List the sample space for the spinner at right. Decide whether each outcome is equally likely to happen.

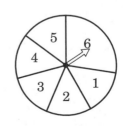

The sample space is 1, 2, 3, 4, 5, 6.

The area of the part labeled 6 is much larger than the others.

The outcomes are not equally likely to happen.

A bag contains 8 marbles of the same size and weight: 3 blue (B), 3 red (R), and 2 purple (P). One marble is chosen at random.

Example 1: List the sample space.

The sample space is B, B, B, R, R, R, P, P.

Example 2: Tell whether the chance of choosing a blue marble is equal to the chance of choosing a red marble.

There are 3 blue marbles and 3 red marbles.

The chance is the same.

Example 3: Is the chance of choosing a blue marble equal to the chance of choosing a purple marble?

There are 3 blue marbles and 2 purple marbles.

The chance is not the same.

Focus on the Idea

To determine whether a game is fair, list all possible outcomes. It is fair if each player's event is equally likely to occur, or each has the same chance of winning.

Practice *Show your work on a separate sheet of paper.*
Write the sample space for each game.

1. Toss a coin.

2. Pick a letter from the word RANDOM.

3. Toss an 8-sided block numbered 1–8.

4. Pick a marble from a jar containing 3 red and 2 white marbles.

5. Spin the spinner to the right.

6. Pick a letter from the word SCHOOL.

Apply the Idea

7. Dina and Tamika are playing a board game using 2 numbered cubes, one red and one white, each labeled 1–6. To help decide which player goes first, they toss the cubes and add the 2 numbers that come up. If their sum is even, Dina gets to go first. If their sum is an odd number, Tamika goes first. List all the outcomes, then determine whether the game is fair.

Write About It

8. Both blocks have the same number of sides with the same number of dots. Write about why one is fair and the other is not fair.

9.2 Finding the Probability of Events

In This Lesson, You Will Learn
To find the probability of an event

Words to Learn
Probability the chance of an event occurring; the ratio of the number of favorable outcomes in the event to the number of possible outcomes

Favorable outcome an outcome in the event you want

Erik is playing a game at a carnival. Erik reaches his hand into a box that contains 9 ping-pong balls, numbered 2 through 10. If he picks the 10, he wins a ticket for a free ride. If he picks any other number, he loses. What is his chance of winning?

New Idea

The chance of something happening is called its **probability**. The probability of an event is written as a ratio of the number of **favorable outcomes**, or ways to win, to the total number of possible outcomes. In Erik's game there is only 1 favorable outcome, or 1 way to win: He needs to pick the 10. There are 9 possible outcomes: 2, 3, 4, 5, 6, 7, 8, 9, 10. To find the probability, write the ratio.

$$\text{Probability} = \frac{\text{Number of favorable outcomes}}{\text{Number of possible outcomes}} = \frac{1}{9}$$

Example 1: The letters of the word ALPHABET are written on cards. One lettered card is chosen at random. Find the probability of choosing a vowel.

Step 1: List and count the possible outcomes.   A, L, P, H, A, B, E, T; 8 total

Step 2: List and count the favorable outcomes.   A, A, E; 3 total

Step 3: Write the ratio of the number of favorable outcomes to possible outcomes. $\frac{3}{8}$

The probability of choosing a vowel is $\frac{3}{8}$.

Example 2: A jar contains 5 coins: a penny (1¢), 2 nickels (5¢), 1 dime (10¢), and 1 quarter (25¢). Find the probability of picking a coin worth more than 6 cents.

Step 1: List and count the possible outcomes.   1¢, 5¢, 5¢, 10¢, 25¢; 5 total

Step 2: List and count the favorable outcomes.   10¢, 25¢; 2 total

Step 3: Write the ratio of the number of favorable $\dfrac{2}{5}$
outcomes to possible outcomes.

The probability of choosing a coin worth
more than 6 cents is $\dfrac{2}{5}$.

The smallest probability is zero. An event with a probability of
zero is impossible. The largest probability is 1. An event with a
probability of 1 will always happen.

Example: A cube labeled with the numbers 1–6
is tossed.

Find the probability that the cube lands on 8.   There are no 8s.
The probability of tossing an 8 is zero. $\dfrac{0}{6} = 0$

Find the probability that the cube lands on   All the numbers are
a number less than 7.   less than seven.

The probability of tossing a number less $\dfrac{6}{6} = 1$
than 7 is 1.

Focus on the Idea

To find the probability of an event, write the ratio of the number of
favorable outcomes to the number of possible outcomes. A
probability of 0 means an event is impossible. A probability of 1
means an event will always happen.

Practice *Show your work on a separate sheet of paper.*

Find the probability of each event.

1. Toss a number cube labeled 1–6.

    a. toss a 5   **b.** toss an even number
    c. toss a 6   **d.** toss a number greater than 4
    e. toss an odd number   **f.** toss a number less than 10

2. Spin the spinner at the right.

    a. land on red   **b.** land on green
    c. land on blue   **d.** land on purple

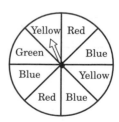

Apply the Idea

3. Johanna buys 5 tickets to a raffle. 100 tickets are sold in all.
    What is the probability that she wins?

Write About It

4. A store is giving away 50 balloons. 10 of them have coupons inside.
    Explain how to find the chance that you pick a balloon with a coupon?

9.3 Making Tree Diagrams

In This Lesson, You Will Learn

To make a tree diagram

To read a tree diagram to list possible outcomes

Words to Learn

Tree diagram a diagram used to show all possible outcomes

An ice cream shop makes sundaes with one of 2 flavors of ice cream (vanilla or chocolate), one of 2 sauces (fudge or butterscotch), and one of 2 toppings (jimmies or whipped cream). Every time he goes to the ice cream shop, Lamal tries a different sundae. How many possible sundae combinations are there in all?

New Idea

To choose a sundae, Lamal has to make three choices: an ice cream, a sauce, and a topping. Each choice has its own outcomes. One way to find all the possible combinations of outcomes is to make a **tree diagram**. List the first choices (ice cream flavor) and from each of these choices draw lines, called branches, to list the next choices (sauces). Then from each of these branches draw branches to list the next choices (topping).

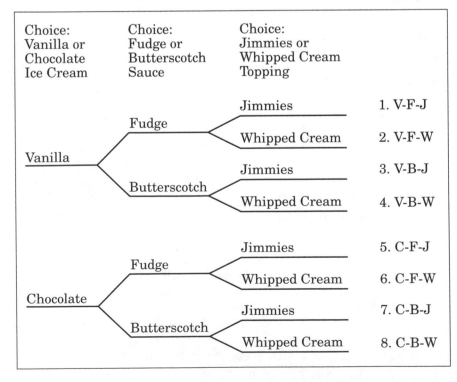

Choice: Vanilla or Chocolate Ice Cream	Choice: Fudge or Butterscotch Sauce	Choice: Jimmies or Whipped Cream Topping	
Vanilla	Fudge	Jimmies	1. V-F-J
		Whipped Cream	2. V-F-W
	Butterscotch	Jimmies	3. V-B-J
		Whipped Cream	4. V-B-W
Chocolate	Fudge	Jimmies	5. C-F-J
		Whipped Cream	6. C-F-W
	Butterscotch	Jimmies	7. C-B-J
		Whipped Cream	8. C-B-W

There are 8 final branches so there are 8 possible combinations. To read the tree diagram, start at a point on the left and follow a branch to its end on the right. For instance, one possible combination is vanilla, butterscotch, and whipped cream (VBW).

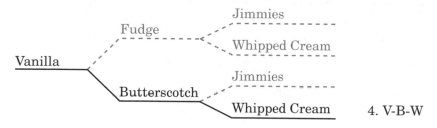

4. V-B-W

Focus on the Idea

To make a tree diagram of possible combinations of outcomes, list the first possible outcomes. From each of these, draw branches to show the next possible outcomes. Continue until there are no more outcomes.

Practice *Show your work on a separate sheet of paper.*
Use the tree diagram to answer Problems 1–4.

1. What is the first choice you make? 2. What is the second choice you make?

3. How many possible choices do you have? 4. List the possible choices.

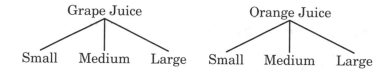

Apply the Idea

5. You can order one meal and one drink from the menu at right.
   a. Make a tree diagram to show the choices you have.
   b. List all of the possible combinations of choices.

Today's Menu	
Meals	Drinks
hamburger	juice
hot dog	milk
taco	

Write About It

6. Think about a situation from your daily life where you make a combination of choices with different possible outcomes; for example, what shoes and jacket to wear in the morning or where and with whom you will eat lunch. Pick a situation and make a tree diagram that shows the possible combinations of outcomes.

9.4 Multiplying to Find the Number of Possible Outcomes

In This Lesson, You Will Learn

To find the number of possible outcomes by multiplying

Carrie is throwing a pizza party during the Super Bowl. She wants to get as many different kinds of pizza as possible. Her favorite pizza parlor offers 2 different crusts (thick or thin), and 3 toppings (sausage, peppers, or mushrooms). How many different combinations of one crust and one topping can she order?

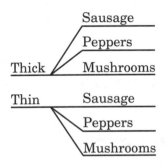

New Idea

To find the number of different pizza combinations, you could draw a tree diagram to list and then count the different combinations. From the diagram you can see that there are 6 different pizza combinations.

There is a shortcut to find the *number* of possible combinations when you do not need to know what the combinations are. Notice that there are 2 crusts and for each crust there are 3 possible toppings. Another way to find the number of combinations is to multiply 2 by 3.

Multiplying the number of choices gives you the number of possible combinations.

Number of first choices
(crusts)
↓
$2 \times 3 = 6$ ← Possible combinations
↑
Number of second choices
(toppings)

Example 1:	Find the number of possible outcomes of tossing a number cube and then tossing a coin.
Step 1:	Find the number of outcomes for the first choice (number cube).
	1, 2, 3, 4, 5, 6; 6 total
Step 2:	Find the number of outcomes for the second choice (coin).
	Heads, Tails; 2 total
Step 3:	Multiply the numbers.
	$6 \times 2 = 12$

There are 12 possible outcomes if you toss a number cube and then toss a coin.

Example 2: Find the number of possible outcomes of tossing a coin 3 times.

Step 1: Find the number of outcomes for the first toss.   H, T; 2 total

Step 2: Find the number of outcomes for the second toss.   H, T; 2 total

Step 3: Find the number of outcomes for the third toss.   H, T; 2 total

Step 4: Multiply. $2 \times 2 \times 2 = 8$

There are 8 possible outcomes if you toss a coin three times.

To find the number of combinations, you need to know only how many choices there are.

Example: Find the number of possible sandwich combinations of 1 bread, 1 meat, and 1 cheese you can make with a choice of 2 breads, 4 meats, and 3 cheeses.

Multiply the number of each choice. $2 \times 4 \times 3 = 24$

There are 24 possible sandwiches.

Focus on the Idea
To find the total number of possible outcomes or combinations, multiply the number of choices.

Practice *Show your work on a separate sheet of paper.*
Find the number of possible outcomes for each.

1. Shirt
   sizes: small, medium, large
   styles: short sleeve, long sleeve

2. Car
   styles: two-door, four-door
   colors: silver, white, blue, black

Apply the Idea
3. You must choose an outfit of a shirt, jeans, socks, and shoes from these items: 4 shirts, 3 pairs of jeans, 6 pairs of socks, and 4 pairs of shoes. How many possible outcomes or combinations can you make?

Write About It
4. A jar contains a red, a blue, and a green marble. If you pull one marble from the jar, hold on to it, and then pick a second marble, how many possible outcomes are there? If you pull one marble from the jar, return it, and then reach in and pull a second marble from the same jar, how many possible outcomes are there? Are there the same number of outcomes in both cases? Explain why or why not.

9.5 Finding the Probability of Independent Events

In This Lesson, You Will Learn

To find the probability of two or more events

Words to Learn

Independent events two or more events whose outcomes do not affect each other

Compound event two or more independent events considered together

---

Liz shows her friends how to play a game with a cube numbered 1–6 and a coin. The first one to roll a 4 and toss a head on the same turn wins. What is the probability of getting a 4 and a head?

New Idea

The two events are **independent events**. The outcome of the number cube roll does not affect the outcome of the coin toss.

1, H	2, H	3, H	4, H	5, H	6, H
1, T	2, T	3, T	4, T	5, T	6, T

One way to find the probability that both events happen is first to list and count all the possible outcomes. Then find the number of ways there are to get the desired outcome.

There is only one way to roll a 4 and then toss a head and there are 12 possible outcomes. The probability is the ratio of number of ways to get 4, H to the number of possible outcomes: $\frac{1}{12}$.

Because the events are independent, there is a faster way of finding the probability of the **compound event** of rolling a 4 and landing on heads. Multiply the probability of the first event by the probability of the second event to get the probability of the compound event.

Probability of first event
(rolling a 4)

$$\frac{1}{6} \times \frac{1}{2} = \frac{1}{12}$$

Probability of second event
(tossing a head)

Example: The letters from the word RED are written on 3 cards and placed in a bag. The letters from the word BLUE are written on 4 cards and placed in another bag. Find the probability of picking an E from the first bag and an E from the second bag.

Step 1: Find the probability of the first event $\frac{1}{3}$ Pick an E from the first bag.

Step 2: Find the probability of the second event $\frac{1}{4}$ Pick an E from the second bag.

Step 3: Multiply the probabilities. $\frac{1}{3} \times \frac{1}{4} = \frac{1}{12}$

The probability of picking an E from the word RED and an E from the word BLUE is $\frac{1}{12}$.

If the events are independent, you can multiply the probabilities of any number of events.

Example: Find the probability of tossing a coin 3 times and having it come up heads, heads, heads.

Step 1: Find the probability of each event. The probability of heads is $\frac{1}{2}$. $\frac{1}{2}, \frac{1}{2}, \frac{1}{2}$

Step 2: Multiply the probabilities. $\frac{1}{2} \times \frac{1}{2} \times \frac{1}{2} = \frac{1}{8}$

The probability of tossing heads three times is $\frac{1}{8}$.

Focus on the Idea
To find the probability of a compound event, multiply the probabilities of each individual event.

Practice *Show your work on a separate sheet of paper.*
Use the items at right to find the probability of compound event described in Problems 1–6.

1. Toss tails and then roll a 2.

2. Roll an odd number and pick an E from the cards.

3. Toss the coin 3 times and get heads, tails, and heads in that order.

4. Toss the coin 3 times and get heads, heads, and tails in that order.

5. Pick a G from the cards and then roll a 6.

6. Toss tails, pick an F from the cards, and roll a 5.

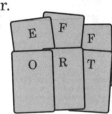

Apply the Idea
7. Look at the map to the right. Joe randomly picks his route from work to Newtown and from Newtown to home. Find the probability that he picks a route that passes both the post office and the restaurant.

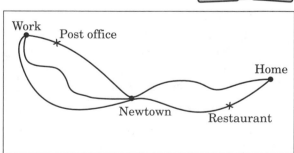

Write About It
8. A jar contains 3 marbles, 2 red and 1 blue. Are picking a red marble from the jar, keeping it, and then picking another red marble from the jar independent events? Explain your answer.

In this chapter, you have learned
- To find the sample space of a game
- To decide whether a game is fair
- To find the probability of an event
- To make a tree diagram
- To read a tree diagram to list possible outcomes
- To find the number of possible outcomes by multiplying
- To find the probability of two or more events

Words You Know

From the lists of Words to Learn, choose the word or phrase that best completes each statement.

1. ___ is the chance of an event occurring.

2. The result of an activity, experiment, or game, is called the ___.

3. The ___ is the list of all possible outcomes of an activity.

4. ___ are two or more events in which the outcome of one event does not affect the outcome of another event.

5. A game in which each player has an equal chance of winning is called a ___.

More Practice   *Show your work on a separate sheet of paper.*
Find the probability of each event.

6. Toss a cube with sides numbered 1–6.
   a. toss a 2
   b. toss a 2 or a 4
   c. toss a 1, 3, or 5
   d. toss an even number
   e. toss an even or an odd number
   f. toss a 7

7. Spin the spinner shown at the right.
   a. land on blue
   b. land on 6
   c. land on a color
   d. land on an even number
   e. land on a number
   f. land on a number greater than 3

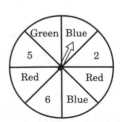

Answer the following questions Involving tree diagrams.

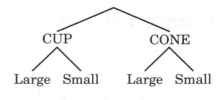

8. Look at the tree diagram on the right.

   a. List all the possible combinations of choices.

   b. For what could this be a tree diagram?

9. Make a tree diagram to show the possible outcomes if you toss a coin three times.

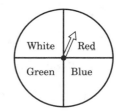

10. Draw a tree diagram to list all the possible outcomes if you spin the spinner at the right and then toss a coin.

Find the number of possible outcomes using the number of choices for each item.

11. Car
    6 exterior colors
    5 interior colors

12. Bicycle helmet
    4 colors
    3 sizes
    2 styles

13. Lilly can take the 1, 2, 3, or 9 train from 96th Street to 42nd Street. From 42nd Street she can take either the N or the R train to 23rd Street. How many ways are there to go from 96th Street to 23rd Street by train?

Problems You Can Solve

Use the items at right to find the probability of the compound events described in Problems 14–18.

14. Toss heads with the coin and pick a blue marble from the jar.

15. Pick a red marble from the jar and pick the letter *E* from the cards.

16. Toss tails with the coin and pick a vowel from the cards.

17. Toss heads with the coin, pick a blue marble from the jar, and toss heads again.

18. Pick a green marble from the jar and pick the letter *F* from the cards.

Chapter 9 Practice Test

1. A jar contains 3 pennies, 2 nickels, and 3 quarters. You pick one at random. Find the probability of each event.

   a. pick a penny

   b. pick a nickel

   c. pick a quarter

   d. pick a coin worth more than 4 cents

   e. pick a coin worth 10 cents

2. A bag contains 12 marbles: 5 red, 5 blue, and 2 white. The white marbles are numbered 1 and 2. The others do not have numbers. You pick one at random. Find the probability of each event.

   a. pick a red marble

   b. pick a blue marble

   c. pick a marble with the number 1

   d. pick a marble with the number 2

   e. pick a white marble

3. An ice cream store offers a choice of 10 flavors and 3 toppings. There are two sizes that you can order in either a cup or a cone. How many different possibilities are there if you can choose 1 flavor, 1 topping, the size, and a cup or a cone?

4. Make a tree diagram to show all the possible outcomes if you first pick a coin from a jar that has a penny, a dime, and a quarter, and then toss the coin.

5. How many different outcomes are possible if you toss a coin, roll a six-sided number cube, and then toss another coin?

6. Use the number cube, the spinner and the cards pictured below to find the probability of the compound events.

   a. roll a 6 with the number cube and spin green

   b. spin blue and pick an *R* from the cards

   c. roll an even number with the number cube and pick an *M* from the cards

   d. roll a 3 with the number cube and then roll 3 again

   e. pick a vowel from the cards, spin red, and roll a 2

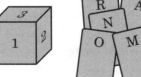

Chapter 10
Integers

In this chapter, you will learn

- To identify integers as positive or negative numbers
- To compare integers
- To find the absolute value of an integer
- To add integers
- To subtract integers
- To multiply integers
- To divide integers

The chart at right shows the high and low temperatures and the average wind chill temperature for three winter days in a big Midwestern city. When you measure temperature in positive and negative numbers, you are working with integers. Understanding how to compare, add, subtract, multiply, and divide integers can help you answer questions such as: Which day has the warmest temperature? If the temperature is 6°, rises 2°, climbs another 3°, then drops 12°, what is the temperature? If the temperature drops at a rate of 3° an hour, what is the change in temperature after 4 hours? What is the difference between the high and low temperatures on Monday? What is the average daily low for the 3 days shown?

Whenever you indicate ups and downs, gains and losses, or above and below, you are using positive and negative numbers. In this chapter, you will learn the skills you need to answer questions such as these as we look at examples of how integers are used in situations related to life in the city.

Temperatures

	Mon.	Tues.	Wed.
High	15°	28°	31°
Low	−10°	−2°	3°
Wind Chill	−19°	−10°	1°

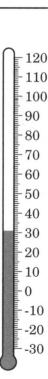

10.1 Writing and Comparing Integers

In This Lesson, You Will Learn

To identify integers as positive or negative numbers

To compare integers

To find the absolute value of an integer

Words to Learn

Positive numbers the numbers to the right of zero on a number line. Positive numbers have values greater than 0.

Negative numbers the numbers to the left of zero on a number line. Negative numbers have values less than 0.

Integers the numbers: . . . ⁻4, ⁻3, ⁻2, ⁻1, 0, 1, 2, 3, 4 . . .

Opposite numbers two numbers the same distance from zero in opposite directions on a number line

Absolute value a number's distance from zero on a number line

---

Mimi is standing on the corner of a city block. The fruit store is 2 blocks east and the bookstore is 2 blocks west. These stores are 2 blocks away, but not in the same direction. How can Mimi use numbers to show the distance and direction of each store?

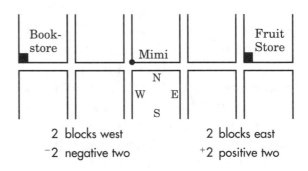

2 blocks west
⁻2 negative two

2 blocks east
⁺2 positive two

New Idea

You can use positive and negative numbers to represent numbers in opposite directions. **Positive numbers** appear to the right of zero on a number line and **negative numbers** appear to the left of zero.

Positive and negative whole numbers are called **integers**, or signed numbers. Every number, except zero, has a sign. If no sign appears in front of a number, it is positive. You can extend the number line of whole numbers to show all the integers, including the negative numbers. Positive numbers are greater than zero. Negative numbers are less than zero.

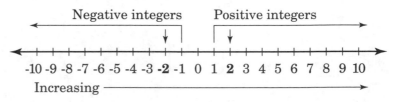

2 and $^-2$ are called **opposite numbers**. They are the same distance from zero but in opposite directions. They have the same **absolute value**. Absolute value is a *distance*, so it is always positive.

$|^+2|$ → the absolute value of $^+2$ is 2

$|^-2|$ → the absolute value of $^-2$ is 2

$|\quad|$ means the absolute value of the number inside.

You can use integers to describe many situations. *Negative* usually means *down, decrease, below,* or *loss.* Positive usually implies *up, increase, above,* or *gain.*

Example: Use an integer to describe each situation.

loss of 5 yards	$^-5$	3 minutes ago	$^-3$
up 10 points	$^+10$	no change in altitude	0

You can use a number line to compare the values of integers. Numbers increase in value to the right.

Example: Compare the following pairs of numbers.

3, $^-10$	3 is greater than $^-10$.
$^-4$, $^-1$	$^-4$ is less than $^-1$.
0, $^-8$	0 is greater than $^-8$.

Focus on the Idea

Integers are positive and negative whole numbers. Negative numbers are to the left of zero on a number line and positive numbers are to the right of zero.

Practice *Show your work on a separate sheet of paper.*

Name the opposite of each integer.

1. 4   2. $^-3$ 3. $^+15$ 4. $^-1$

Find the absolute value of each.

5. $|^-5|$ 6. $|^+3|$ 7. $|7|$ 8. $|0|$

Compare each pair of integers.

9. 3, $^-3$ 10. $^-9$, $^-3$ 11. 0, $^-5$ 12. $^-54$, 1   13. 4, $^+4$

Apply the Idea

Use an integer to describe each situation.

14. 4 meters below sea level   15. gain 6 pounds   16. no change in value

Write About It

17. Explain why $^-99$ is less than $^-9$, and $^-9$ is less than 0.

↳ 10.2 Adding Integers

In This Lesson, You Will Learn
To add integers

Allison, Max, Kara, and Dave live in a large, modern apartment building. Coming in from school one afternoon, the friends meet at the ground floor elevators. Allison goes up 3 floors and then up 5 more. Max goes down 1 floor and then down another. Kara goes up 7 floors to return a book to a friend and then down 3. Dave goes up 4 floors to get his car keys and then down 6. Where is each of them when he or she stops?

Floor 12	
Floor 11	
Floor 10	
Floor 9	
Floor 8	
Floor 7	
Floor 6	
Floor 5	
Floor 4	
Floor 3	
Floor 2	
Floor 1	
Ground floor	
Parking level 1	
Parking level 2	
Parking level 3	

New Idea

You can represent the movements of the elevator as integers and combine them in addition problems that you can solve using a number line. They all started at the ground floor, 0. Use $^+$ for up and $^-$ for down. Parentheses are often used around a signed number to keep the sign of the number separate from the operation sign.

From Allison and Max's movements you can see the rule for adding integers with the same sign.

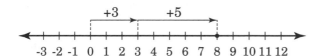

Allison: $(^+3) + (^+5) = {}^+8$

Allison ends 8 floors above the ground floor.

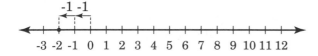

Max: $(^-1) + (^-1) = {}^-2$

Max ends 2 floors below the ground floor.

To add integers with the same sign, add their absolute values. Make the sum the same sign as the integers.

Example: Add $(^-2) + (^-4)$.

    Step 1:   Determine the sign of the sum. $(^-2) + (^-4) = ^-$

                    Signs are the same, so keep the
same sign as the integers.

    Step 2:   Add the absolute values. $2 + 4 = 6$

                    $(^-2) + (^-4) = ^-6$

Kara and Dave's motion shows the rule for adding integers with different signs.

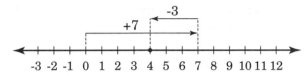

      Kara: $(^+7) + (^-3) = ^+4$

Kara goes up 4 floors more than she goes down, so she ends 4 floors above ground.

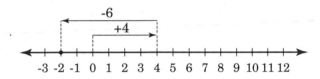

      Dave: $(^+4) + (^-6) = ^-2$

Dave goes down 2 floors more than he goes up, so he ends up 2 floors below ground.

To add integers with different signs, subtract the absolute values and use the sign of the number with the larger absolute value.

Example 1:   Add $(^-10) + (3)$.

    Step 1:   Determine the sign of the sum. $(^-10) + (3) = ^-$
                    Signs are different, so use the sign
of the number with the larger
absolute value.

    Step 2:   Subtract the absolute values. $10 - 3 = 7$

                    $(^-10) + (3) = ^-7$

Example 2:   Add $(^-4) + (9)$.

    Step 1:   Determine the sign of the sum. $(^-4) + (9) = ^+$
                    Signs are different, so use the sign
of the number with the larger
absolute value.

    Step 2:   Subtract the absolute values. $9 - 4 = 5$

                    $(^-4) + (9) = ^+5$

The sum of opposites is always 0.

Example: Add $(^-2) + (2)$.

The signs are different and the numbers have the same absolute value.

$2 - 2 = 0$

$(^-2) + (2) = 0$

✓ Check the Math

Jorge lost 6 yards on his first play of the football game, then gained 3 yards in his second play, and gained another 4 yards by the end of the quarter. Jorge's coach told him that he ended up losing 1 yard for the quarter. Is the coach correct? Why or why not?

Focus on the Idea

To add integers with the same sign, add their absolute values. Make the sum the same sign as the integers. To add integers with different signs, subtract the absolute values and use the sign of the number with the larger absolute value.

Practice *Show your work on a separate sheet of paper.*

Determine the sign of each sum.

1. $(^-12) + (10)$ 2. $(^-6) + (^-20)$ 3. $(111) + (^-55)$ 4. $(^-28) + (56)$

Add.

5. $(^-13) + (^-3)$ 6. $(^+8) + (^-10)$ 7. $(^+4) + (^-2)$ 8. $(^-2) + (^-8)$

9. $(^-5) + (5)$ 10. $(^-4) + (^-4)$ 11. $(^+6) + (^+4)$ 12. $(9) + (^-15)$

13. $(^-22) + (0)$ 14. $(^-15) + (20)$ 15. $(^+12) + (^-12)$ 16. $(^-24) + (4)$

17. $(18) + (^+2)$ 18. $(^-10) + (^-30)$ 19. $(33) + (^-48)$ 20. $(^-27) + (23)$

Extend the Idea

When you add more than two integers, you may find it easier to regroup the numbers so that you add numbers with the same sign first.

Example 1: Add $(^-4) + (^+10) + (^-5) + (^+3)$.

Step 1: Regroup the numbers so that integers with the same signs are together.

$\underbrace{(^-4) + (^-5)} + \underbrace{(^+10) + (^+3)}$

Step 2: Add the numbers with the same signs.

$(^-9) \quad + \quad (^+13)$

Step 3: Add the numbers with different signs.

$(^-9) \quad + \quad (^+13) = {}^+4$

$(^-4) + (^+10) + (^-5) + (^+3) = 4$

Example 2: Add $(12) + (^-18) + (^-6) + (10)$.

Step 1: Regroup the numbers. $(12) + (10) + (^-18) + (^-6)$

Step 2: Add the numbers with the same signs. $(22) \quad + \quad (^-24)$

Step 3: Add the numbers with different signs. $(22) \quad + \quad (^-24) = ^-2$

$(12) + (^-18) + (^-6) + (10) = ^-2$

You do not have to regroup the numbers first. Sometimes the integers combine in ways that make it is easier to just add from left to right.

Example: Add $(^-8) + (^-2) + (10) + (^-6)$.

Add from left to right.

$$\underbrace{(^-8) + (^-2)} + (10) + (^-6)$$
$$\underbrace{(^-10) \quad + (10)} + (^-6)$$
$$0 \qquad + (^-6) = ^-6$$

$(^-8) + (^-2) + (10) + (^-6) = ^-6$

Practice *Show your work on a separate sheet of paper.*
Add.

21. $(^-15) + (^-3) + (^-2)$

22. $(7) + (^-14) + (^-10) + (13)$

23. $(^-9) + (11) + (^-4)$

24. $(^-12) + (10) + (^-8) + (^-12)$

25. $(25) + (^-38) + (12) + (^-6)$

26. $(^-26) + (^-14) + (10)$

27. $(^-5) + (^-20) + (10)$

28. $(^-14) + (^-6) + (9) + (11)$

29. $(^-6) + (^-10) + (^-8)$

Apply the Idea
30. Laurie goes to the ATM machine on Monday and withdraws $75 from her savings account. She withdraws another $20 on Thursday. On Friday, she cashes her paycheck and deposits $100 in her savings account. What is the overall change in her savings account balance for the week?

31. The stock market climbs 29 points in one day. The next day it dips 31 points, then climbs a modest 3 points the day after. What is the change in the market over the 3-day period?

32. A hot air balloon rises 300 feet, descends 500 feet, and then rises 50 feet. What is the total change?

✏ Write About It
33. Make up a word problem to go with the problem $(10) + (^-3) + (^-9)$.

⬥ **10.3** Subtracting Integers

In This Lesson, You Will Learn
To subtract integers

Chris competes on a diving team. The diving end of the swimming pool where the team practices is 12 feet below ground. The diving board is 14 feet above the ground. How far is the distance from the top of the diving board to the bottom of the pool?

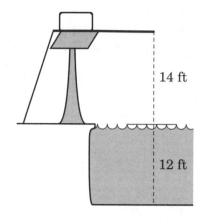

14 ft

12 ft

New Idea

The elevation of the diving board is $^+14$ feet, and the elevation of the bottom of the pool is $^-12$ feet. You can use a number line to find the difference between $^+14$ feet and $^-12$ feet, rather than subtracting. The difference between the two integers is the distance between them.

From $^-12$ to 0 is 12 feet. From 0 to $^+14$ is another 14 feet. The total distance between the numbers is 26 feet. The difference between $^+14$ feet and $^-12$ feet is 26 feet.

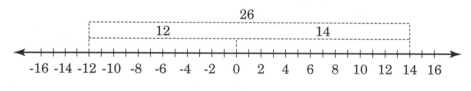

$$(^+14) - (^-12) = {^+26}$$

You usually subtract to find the difference between two known distances. You also can solve any subtraction problem by changing it to an addition problem. By looking at the 2 math sentences to the right, you can see that subtracting a number is the same as adding its opposite.

$$9 - 5 = 4$$
$$9 + (^-5) = 4$$

You can use this idea to subtract integers. Change the operation from subtraction to addition and change the sign of the second number to its opposite.

Example 1: Subtract $(^+14) - (^-12)$.

    Step 1: Change the operation to addition. Change the sign of the second number. $(^+14) + (^+12)$

    Step 2: Follow the rules for addition. If signs are the same, keep the sign. Add the absolute values. $(^+14) + (^+12) = 26$

               $(^+14) - (^-12) = 26$

Example 2: Subtract $(^-8) - (^-3)$.

    Step 1: Change the operation to addition. $(^-8) + (^+3)$
               Change the sign of the second number.

    Step 2: Follow the rules for addition. The signs $(^-8) + (^+3) = ^-5$
               are different. Subtract the absolute
               values and use the sign of the number
               with the larger absolute value.

               $(^-8) - (^-3) = ^-5$

Example 3: Subtract $4 - 10$.

    Step 1: Change the operation to addition.
               Change the sign of the second number. $4 + (^-10)$

    Step 2: Follow the rules for addition. The signs
               are different. Subtract the absolute $4 + (^-10) = ^-6$
               values and use the sign of the number
               with the larger absolute value.

               $4 - 10 = ^-6$

Focus on the Idea

To subtract an integer, add the opposite of the integer.

Practice. *Show your work on a separate sheet of paper.*

Subtract.

1. $(^-7) - (12)$
2. $(^-8) - (^-3)$
3. $(9) - (^-15)$
4. $24 - 16$
5. $13 - 15$
6. $(^-14) - (^-20)$
7. $(37) - (^-13)$
8. $(^-19) - (^-19)$
9. $(15) - (^-15)$
10. $0 - 14$
11. $(^-25) - (^-15)$
12. $5 - 10$

Apply the Idea

13. Keesha's office is on the 14th floor of her building. She parks her car on Level D, 4 floors below ground level. How many floors down does Keesha have to go to get from her office to her car?

14. As part of an economics project, Tamara is tracking how much money she would win or lose if she were to buy and sell certain stocks. Tamara makes $54 on her first imaginary stock transaction. She loses $75 on her next stock trade. By how much is she up or down? Write your answer as a signed number.

Write About It

15. Draw a picture to show how to subtract $(^+10) - (^-7)$.

⬇ 10.4 Multiplying Integers

In This Lesson, You Will Learn
To multiply integers

Words to Learn
Unlike signs signs that are different from each other
Like signs signs that are alike: both negative or both positive

---

Kelly's family is moving out of their old apartment and into a new building. The movers load their furniture into the freight elevator. The elevator descends 4 floors a minute. How many floors does the elevator travel if the trip takes 3 minutes?

New Idea

The elevator goes down 4 floors each minute. You can use the integer $^-4$ to represent the movement. To calculate how far it moves in 3 minutes, multiply $^-4$ by 3.

$$(3) \times (^-4) = ?$$

3 and $^-4$ have **unlike signs**. To find the product of two unlike signs you can write the problem as repeated addition. Add $^-4$ three times.

$$(^-4) + (^-4) + (^-4) = {}^-12 \quad \text{so} \quad (3) \times (^-4) = {}^-12$$

The elevator traveled 12 floors down in 3 minutes.

The product of a positive and a negative is always negative. This is true no matter in what order the numbers appear. $(^-4) \times (3) = {}^-12$

To discover the sign of the product of two **like signs**, look for a pattern in simple facts you know.

As the numbers on the left decrease by 1, the numbers on the right increase by 3. Continuing the pattern, you see that the product of two negatives is positive.

$$
\begin{array}{l}
\ \ (3) \times (^-3) = {}^-9 \\
-1\ \ (2) \times (^-3) = {}^-6 \quad +3\\
-1\ \ (1) \times (^-3) = {}^-3 \quad +3\\
-1\ \ (0) \times (^-3) = 0 \quad +3\\
-1\ (^-1) \times (^-3) = 3 \quad +3 \ \rightarrow \ \text{negative} \times \text{negative} = \text{positive}
\end{array}
$$

Example 1: Multiply $(^-4) \times (^-2)$.

The signs are like. The product is positive.

$$(^-4) \times (^-2) = 8$$

Example 2: Multiply $(5) \times (^-3)$.

The signs are unlike. The product is negative.

$(5) \times (^-3) = ^-15$

Example 3: Multiply $(^-7) \times 0$.

The product of 0 and any number is 0. Zero does not have a sign.

$(^-7) \times 0 = 0$

Example 4: Multiply $(^-1) \times (^-3) \times (^-2)$.

Multiply from left to right.

$$\underbrace{(^-1) \times (^-3)}_{(^+3)} \times (^-2)$$
$$(^+3) \quad \times (^-2) = ^-6$$

$(^-1) \times (^-3) \times (^-2) = ^-6$

Focus on the Idea

The product of two integers with unlike signs is negative. The product of two integers with like signs is positive.

Practice *Show your work on a separate sheet of paper.*

Tell whether the product is negative or positive.

1. $(^-43) \times (^-22)$ **2.** $(2) \times (^-31)$ **3.** $(^-1) \times (543)$ **4.** $(^-13) \times (^-65)$

Multiply.

5. $(^-7) \times 3$ **6.** $(^-9) \times (^-9)$ **7.** $(4) \times (6)$ **8.** $(^-11) \times (^+3)$

9. $(^-4) \times (12)$ **10.** $(^-1) \times (1)$ **11.** $(5) \times (^-5)$ **12.** $(0) \times (^-13)$

13. $(^+15) \times (^-3)$ **14.** $(^-32) \times 3$ **15.** $(^-16) \times (^-16)$ **16.** $(10) \times (^-9)$

17. $(^-3) \times (^-2) \times (^+4)$ **18.** $(^-5) \times (3) \times (^-6)$

Apply the Idea

19. The temperature has been dropping 2 degrees each hour and is now 0 degrees.

a. If the temperature continues to drop at the same rate, what will the temperature be in 4 hours?

b. What was the temperature 3 hours ago?

Write About It

20. Explain what the math sentence $(^-2) \times (^-3) = 6$ could mean.

10.5 Dividing Integers

In This Lesson, You Will Learn
To divide integers

Words to Learn
Divisor the number used to divide
Quotient the answer you get when you divide
Dividend the number to be divided

A security guard walks down 12 flights of stairs in 6 minutes. On average, how many flights of stairs per minute does he walk?

New Idea
To find the number of flights the guard walks per minute, you divide the total (12) by the minutes (6).

12 flights ÷ 6 minutes = 2 flights per minute

But this equation does not tell you that the guard went down, not up. Use negatives to show the downward direction he was traveling.

$(^-12) \div (^+6) = {}^-2$

This equation now shows that a negative divided by a positive is negative. You can check this by multiplying. Multiply the **divisor** by the **quotient**. The answer should be the **dividend**.

$(^-2) \times (^+6) = {}^-12$

All division problems have a related multiplication problem. You can use the rules for multiplication to find the other rules for division.

$(^-2) \times (^+6) = {}^-12 \rightarrow (^-12) \div (^+6) = {}^-2 \rightarrow$ negative ÷ positive = negative

$(^-4) \times (^-5) = {}^+20 \rightarrow (^+20) \div (^-5) = {}^-4 \rightarrow$ positive ÷ negative = negative

$(^+3) \times (^+2) = {}^+6 \rightarrow (^+6) \div (^+2) = {}^+3 \rightarrow$ positive ÷ positive = positive

$(^+10) \times (^-3) = {}^-30 \rightarrow (^-30) \div (^-3) = {}^+10 \rightarrow$ negative ÷ negative = positive

From the list, you see that the rules for dividing integers are similar to the rules for multiplication.

Example 1: Divide $(^-24) \div (^-6)$.

The signs are like. The quotient is positive.

$(^-24) \div (^-6) = 4$

Example 2: Divide $(12) \div (^-4)$.

The signs are unlike. The quotient is negative.

$(12) \div (^-4) = ^-3$

Example 3: Divide $(^-15) \div (15)$.

The signs are unlike. The quotient is negative.

$(^-15) \div (15) = ^-1$

Example 4: Divide $0 \div (^-4)$

Zero divided by any number is zero.

$0 \div (^-4) = 0$

Focus on the Idea

The quotient of integers with like signs is positive. The quotient of integers with unlike signs is negative.

Practice *Show your work on a separate sheet of paper.*

Tell whether each quotient is positive or negative.

1. $(^-50) \div (^-2)$ **2.** $128 \div (^-7)$ **3.** $(^-1,800) \div (24)$

Write the related division problem for each multiplication problem.

4. $(^-6) \times (2) = ^-12$ **5.** $(8) \times (^-8) = ^-64$ **6.** $(^-5) \times (^-4) = 20$

Divide.

7. $(^-25) \div (5)$ **8.** $(^-66) \div (^-11)$ **9.** $(^+13) \div (^-1)$ **10.** $(50) \div (^+25)$

11. $(^-24) \div (^-24)$ **12.** $(^-28) \div (7)$ **13.** $(^+10) \div (^-2)$ **14.** $(^-4) \div (^-1)$

15. $(48) \div (^-16)$ **16.** $(^+56) \div (^+4)$ **17.** $(^-12) \div (12)$ **18.** $(^-64) \div (^-8)$

Apply the Idea

19. David decides to go on a diet. In the first month, he loses 15 pounds, in the second month he gains 2 pounds, and in the third month he loses another 5 pounds. What is his average monthly weight change?

20. A plane descends 2,340 feet in 10 minutes. What is the average change in the plane's altitude each minute?

Write About It

21. Explain how the rules for multiplying integers and dividing integers are related.

In this chapter, you have learned

- To identify integers as positive or negative numbers
- To compare integers
- To find the absolute value of an integer
- To add integers
- To subtract integers
- To multiply integers
- To divide integers

Words You Know

From the lists of Words to Learn, choose the word or phrase that best completes each statement.

1. The ___ are the numbers greater than zero on a number line.

2. Two numbers the same distance from zero in opposite directions on a number line are ___ .

3. The ___ are the numbers . . . ⁻4, ⁻3, ⁻2, ⁻1, 0, 1, 2, 3, 4 . . .

4. The ___ of a number is its distance from zero.

5. The numbers less than zero on a number line are ___ .

More Practice *Show your work on a separate sheet of paper.*
Use an integer to describe each situation.

6. 45 meters below sea level

7. altitude of 2,356 meters

8. gained 25 yards

9. owe $150

10. dropped 62 feet

11. temperature rose 12°

Name the opposite of each integer.

12. ⁺35

13. ⁻42

14. ⁻75

15. 30

Compare each pair of integers.

16. 0, ⁻7

17. ⁻10, ⁻2

18. 3, ⁻12

19. ⁻5, ⁻9

Find the absolute value of each.

20. $|{}^-12|$

21. $|{}^+7|$

22. $|4|$

23. $|{}^-33|$

Add.

24. $(^-13) + (^-13)$ **25.** $(16) + (^-4)$ **26.** $(^-28) + (28)$ **27.** $(^-14) + (7)$

28. $45 + 15$ **29.** $(^-29) + (21)$ **30.** $(100) + (^-25)$ **31.** $(^-68) + (^-32)$

32. $(5) + (^-19) + (^-4)$ **33.** $(^-5) + (^-5) + (^-10)$ **34.** $(^-3) + (5) + (9) + (^-11)$

Subtract.

35. $(^-10) - (^-5)$ **36.** $(^-16) - (^-20)$ **37.** $(8) - (^-9)$ **38.** $(25) - (^-5)$

39. $(^-3) - (^-3)$ **40.** $(^-18) - (^-4)$ **41.** $(6) - (^-4)$ **42.** $8 - 9$

43. $(^-24) - (24)$ **44.** $(^-28) - (^-40)$ **45.** $10 - 20$ **46.** $(^-8) - (^-6)$

Multiply.

47. $(^-8) \times (3)$ **48.** $(7) \times (^-4)$ **49.** $(^-5) \times (^-6)$ **50.** $(^-2) \times (^-2)$

51. $(^-1) \times (6)$ **52.** $(^-9) \times (^-10)$ **53.** $0 \times (^-8)$ **54.** $(^-12) \times (5)$

55. $(^-8) \times (2) \times (^-5)$ **56.** $(^-3) \times (^-3) \times (^-3)$ **57.** $(4) \times (^-5) \times (7)$

Divide.

58. $(20) \div (^-4)$ **59.** $(^-21) \div (^-7)$ **60.** $(^-9) \div (^-3)$ **61.** $(45) \div (^-1)$

62. $(^-32) \div (^-8)$ **63.** $(^-11) \div (11)$ **64.** $(30) \div (6)$ **65.** $(16) \div (^-4)$

Add, subtract, multiply, or divide.

66. $(^-4) + (8)$ **67.** $(^-12) \times (2)$ **68.** $(^-5) - (^-15)$ **69.** $(^-18) \div (^+3)$

70. $(^-9) - (^-4)$ **71.** $(^-8) + (^-7)$ **72.** $(^-6) \times (^-8)$ **73.** $2 - 8$

Problems You Can Solve

The chart at right shows the high and low temperatures and average wind chill temperature for 3 days. Use the information in the chart as needed to answer Problems 74–79.

74. Which day has the warmest wind chill temperature?

75. What is the difference between the high and low temperatures on Monday?

76. What is the difference between the low and wind chill temperatures on Monday?

Temperatures

	Mon.	Tues.	Wed.
High	15°	28°	31°
Low	-10°	-2°	3°
Wind Chill	-19°	-10°	1°

77. What is the average daily low for the 3 days shown?

78. If the temperature is 6°, rises 2°, climbs another 3°, then drops 12°, what is the temperature?

79. If the temperature drops at a rate of 3° an hour, what is the change in temperature after 4 hours?

Use an integer to describe each situation.

1. lose 15 yards
2. gain 16 pounds
3. owe $10
4. drop 50 meters
5. rise 6 points
6. 12 meters below sea level

Name the opposite of each integer.

7. $^-72$
8. $^+54$
9. 20
10. $^-8$

Compare each pair of integers.

11. $^-12, ^-9$
12. $^-1, ^-2$
13. $0, ^-12$
14. $6, ^-19$

Find the absolute value of each.

15. $|14|$
16. $|^-8|$
17. $|^+25|$
18. $|^-22|$

Add.

19. $(^-8) + (^-6)$
20. $(^-10) + (17)$
21. $(6) + (^-14)$
22. $(^-7) + (^+4)$
23. $(^-11) + (33)$
24. $(^-1) + (1)$
25. $(^-14) + (^-36)$
26. $(25) + (^-14)$

Subtract.

27. $(14) - (^-6)$
28. $(^-8) - (8)$
29. $(^-16) - (^-22)$
30. $8 - 13$
31. $(^-17) - (^-17)$
32. $(^-12) - (^-7)$
33. $(^-24) - (^-16)$
34. $0 - (^-8)$

Multiply.

35. $(^-8) \times (^-9)$
36. $(^-3) \times (5)$
37. $(^-6) \times (5)$
38. $(4) \times (^-11)$
39. $(15) \times (^-3)$
40. $(^-10) \times (^-10)$
41. $(^-12) \times (7)$
42. $(^-5) \times (^-13)$

Divide.

43. $(22) \div (^-11)$
44. $(^-48) \div (^-12)$
45. $(^-8) \div (2)$
46. $(25) \div (^-5)$

Perform each operation.

47. $(16) + (^-9)$
48. $(^+4) \times (^-1)$
49. $(^-8) - (^-14)$
50. $(^-52) \div (^-26)$

Use integers to solve.

51. Joe bought his car for $5,500 five years ago. The car is now worth $2,000. On average, how much did the value of the car change per year?

52. Phillipe received a notice from the bank that his account balance was $^-15$ dollars. He immediately deposited $50. During the next week he withdrew $20, deposited $18, and withdrew $30. How much money did he have in his account at the end of the week?

Glossary

A

Absolute value a number's distance from zero on a number line (10.1)

Altitude height (7.3)

Approximate about how many (1.1)

Approximate number an inexact but useful number (2.2)

Area the amount of surface a figure covers (7.2)

At random a condition in which outcomes happen without influence (9.1)

B

Bar graph a graph that uses bars to show a set of data that can be separated into distinct groups (8.3)

Base a side of a polygon (7.2)

Budget a plan for spending money (2.3)

C

Circle a set of points that are all the same distance from a given point, called the center (7.4)

Circle graph a graph that is used to show the relationship of parts of a set of data to the whole set of data (8.5)

Circumference the distance around a circle (7.4)

Common denominator a common multiple of two or more denominators (3.5)

Common multiple a number that is a multiple of two or more different numbers (3.5)

Compound event two or more independent events considered together (9.5)

Cross product the product of the numbers diagonally across from each other in a proportion (5.2)

Cube a rectangular prism with square sides (7.8)

Cubic units volume is measured in cubic units, such as cubic feet, cubic yards, and cubic meters (7.8)

Cylinder a three-dimensional figure with a pair of parallel circular bases of the same size connected by a curved surface (7.8)

D

Data information gathered, usually in the form of numbers (8.1)

Decimal a number written with a dot (2.1)

Decimal point a dot used to separate a whole number from a part less than a whole. Values to the right of the dot are less than 1. (2.1)

Denominator the bottom number of a fraction (3.1)

Diameter a line that passes through the center of the circle and has both its ends on the circle (7.4)

Difference the answer you get when you subtract two numbers (1.2; 2.2)

Digits the 10 basic symbols used to write numbers: 0, 1, 2, 3, 4, 5, 6, 7, 8, 9 (1.1)

Dividend the number to be divided (1.6; 2.6; 10.5)

Divisor the number used to divide (1.6; 2.6; 10.5)

Double to multiply by 2 (4.2)

E

Edge a line where two sides of a prism meet (7.7)

Equivalent fractions fractions that name the same amount (3.3)

Equivalent ratios ratios that have the same value (5.1)

Estimate to find an approximate answer (1.2; 2.2)

Event specific outcome or outcomes (9.1)

F

Faces the flat surfaces or sides of a prism (7.7)

Factor 1. a number multiplied by another number to find a product (1.5) **2.** a whole number that divides into another number with no remainder (3.4)

Fair game a game in which each player has an equal chance of winning (9.1)

Favorable outcome an outcome in the event you want (9.2)

Formula a rule for solving a problem (7.2)

Fraction a number that names part of a whole (3.1)

Frequency table a chart that shows how often a number or item appears in a set of data (8.2)

G

Greatest common factor (GFC) the largest factor that two or more numbers share (3.4)

H

Height the distance between the base and the opposite side. The height makes a right angle with the base. (7.2)

Horizontal axis the line along the bottom of the graph (8.3)

I

Improper fraction a fraction in which the numerator is larger than the denominator (3.2)

Independent events two or more events whose outcomes do not affect each other (9.5)

Integers the numbers: ...$^-4$, $^-3$, $^-2$, $^-1$, 0, 1, 2, 3, 4... (10.1)

Irregular figure any shape that can be broken up into other recognizable shapes (7.6)

L

Like fractions fractions with the same denominators (3.5; 3.6)

Like signs signs that are alike: both negative or both positive (10.4)

Line graph a graph that is used to show continuous change over time (8.4)

Lowest terms a fraction is in lowest terms when the numerator and the denominator of the fraction cannot be divided evenly by any number other than 1 (3.4)

M

Maximum the largest number in a set of data (8.2)

Mean the sum of the data divided by the number of pieces of data (8.1)

Median the middle number when data are ordered from least to greatest (8.1)

Mental math doing arithmetic in your head (1.2)

Minimum the smallest number in a set of data (8.2)

Mixed number a number written with a whole number and a fraction (3.2; 4.2)

Mode the number that appears most often in a set of data (8.1)

Multiple of a number the product of the number and a whole number (3.5)

N

Negative numbers the numbers to the left of zero on a number line. Negative numbers have values less than 0. (10.1)

Numerator the top number of a fraction (3.1)

O

Operation addition, subtraction, multiplication, or division (1.7)

Opposite numbers two numbers the same distance from zero in opposite directions on a number line (10.1)

Order of operations the rules that determine the order in which you add, subtract, multiply, or divide (1.7)

Outcome the result of an activity, experiment, or game (9.1)

P

Parallel lines lines that extend in the same direction and are always the same distance apart (7.1)

Parallelogram a 4-sided polygon whose opposite sides are parallel (7.1)

Parentheses ( ) symbols used to group numbers and operations (1.7)

Partial product the number you get when you multiply a number by one digit of another number (1.5)

Percent a comparison of a number to 100 (6.1)

Perimeter the distance around a figure (7.1)

Pi (π) the ratio of the circumference of a circle to its diameter. The ratio is the same for all circles: π is approximately 3.14 (7.4)

Place value the value of a digit according to its position in a number (1.1)

Polygon a straight-sided, closed, two-dimensional figure with three or more sides. A two-dimensional figure is flat; you can measure it in only two directions. (7.1)

Positive numbers the numbers to the right of zero on a number line. Positive numbers have values greater than 0. (10.1)

Probability the chance of an event occurring; the ratio of the number of favorable outcomes in the event to the number of possible outcomes (9.2)

Product the answer you get when you multiply two or more numbers (1.4; 2.4)

Proportion a statement that says that two ratios have the same value (5.2)

Q

Quotient the answer you get when you divide two numbers (1.4; 2.4; 10.5)

R

r^2 means radius × radius. It does *not* mean radius × 2. (7.5)

Radii the plural form of radius (7.5)

Radius a line segment with one endpoint at the center of a circle and the other endpoint on the circle (7.5)

Rate the cost per unit (2.5)

Rate of exchange the rate for trading money from one country for money from another country (2.5)

Ratio a comparison of two numbers (5.1; 6.1)

Reciprocal numbers two numbers that when multiplied have 1 as their product (4.3)

Rectangle a parallelogram with 4 right angles (7.1)

Rectangular prism a three-dimensional figure with 6 rectangles for sides (7.7)

Regroup to exchange any equivalent amount for another; for example, to exchange a ten for 10 ones or a hundred for 10 tens (1.3)

Remainder the number left over after dividing (1.6)

Right angle an angle that measures 90° (7.1)

Rounding expressing an amount to the nearest ten, hundred, thousand, or other place value (1.1; 2.2)

S

Sample space the list of all possible outcomes of an activity (9.1)

Scale 1. a ratio that compares the measurements in a drawing or model to the actual measurements (5.3) **2.** a series of marks that measure equal distances on a line (8.3)

Scale drawing a drawing that shows an object or distance in proportion to its real measurements (5.3)

Score a piece of data (8.2)

Simplify to write a problem or fraction in lowest terms by dividing by common factors of the numerator and denominator (4.1)

Square a rectangle with 4 equal sides (7.1)

Square units area is measured in square units, such as square inches, square meters, and square miles (7.2)

Statistics the study of data (8.1)

Sum the answer you get when you add two or more numbers (1.2; 2.2)

Surface area the total area of the sides of a three-dimensional figure (7.7)

T

Three-dimensional having length, width, and height. Most objects in real life are three-dimensional. (7.7)

Tree diagram a diagram used to show all possible outcomes (9.3)

Trend pattern of change over time (8.4)

Triangle a polygon with 3 sides (7.1)

U

Unlike fractions fractions with different denominators (3.7)

Unlike signs signs that are different from each other (10.4)

V

Vertical axis the line up the side of the graph (8.3)

Volume the amount of space enclosed by a three-dimensional figure (7.8)

W

Whole numbers the numbers 0, 1, 2, 3, 4, and so on (1.1)

Answer Key

Chapter 1 Whole Numbers

1.1 Rounding Whole Numbers
1. 70 3. 540 5. 1,070 7. 4,010 9. 300
11. 6,000 13. 3,200 15. 70,200 17. 3,000
19. 2,000 21. 3,000 23. 18,000 25. 1,700
27. 2,400

1.2 Estimating Sums and Differences
1. 300 3. 100 5. 300 7. 4,000 9. b. 3,000
11. about 2,000 hot dogs

1.3 Adding and Subtracting Whole Numbers
1. 27 3. 200 5. 201 7. 3,879 9. 715
11. a. 585 cards; b. 650 cards; c. 732 cards
13. 65 cards

1.4 Estimating Products and Quotients
1. 240 3. 3,000 5. 20 7. 20 9. c. 450×80
11. 180 guests 13. $50

1.5 Multiplying Whole Numbers
1. 135 3. 522 5. 2,106 7. 73,788
9. 432 boxes 11. 864 boxes

1.6 Dividing Whole Numbers
1. 32 3. 14 5. 15 7. 412 9. 6 R3
11. 23 13. 14 shelves

1.7 Using the Order of Operations
1. 50 3. 31 5. 22 7. 48 9. 62 11. 7
13. 16 15. 8 17. 0 19. 1,311 21. 168
23. 17 25. 11 27. 1,500
29. $1,280; $40 \times 12 + 100 \times 8$
31. $10; $(3 + 2) \times 2$

Chapter 1 Review
1. quotient 2. approximate
3. order of operations 4. divisor 5. factor
6. Rounding 7. product 8. dividend 9. 20
10. 150 11. 1,030 12. 500 13. 300 14. 400
15. 200 16. 1,400 17. 4,000 18. 2,100
19. 1,000 20. 14,000 21. 4,000 22. 20,000
23. 150; 145 24. 160; 159 25. 160; 158
26. 3,400; 3,435 27. 500; 519 28. 4,000; 4,000
29. 8,900; 8,961 30. 700; 686 31. 100; 126
32. 800; 805 33. 10; 9 R12 34. 2,700; 2,418
35. 7; 7 R24 36. 3,200; 3,760 37. 50; 49 R16
38. 50,000; 49,872 39. 120; 113 R9
40. 128,000; 129,948 41. 600; 557 R13
42. 150,000; 128,260 43. 23 44. 11 45. 21
46. 12 47. 30 48. 50 49. 2 50. 14 51. 29
52. 1 53. 56 54. 4 55. 104 in. 56. 90 heads
57. 25 bags 58. 205 lbs

Chapter 2 Decimals

2.1 Comparing and Ordering Decimals
1. 3.36; 3.59; 3.64 3. 43; 43.022; 43.22
5. 0.004; 0.104; 6.401
7. 1. Marie-José Pérec 22.12; 2. Mary Onyali 22.38; 3. Inger Miller 22.41

2.2 Estimating Sums and Differences of Decimals

1. 159   **3.** 23   **5.** $11   **7.** 5   **9.** 10   **11.** $64
13. 35 miles; 4 miles

2.3 Adding and Subtracting Decimals

1. .78   **3.** 7.4   **5.** 4.86   **7.** $16.01   **9.** 1.77
11. $11.90   **13.** $4.87   **15.** $13.10
17. $29; $29.09   **19.** $62; $62.52

2.4 Estimating Products and Quotients of Decimals

1. $150   **3.** $4   **5.** 3 pies

2.5 Multiplying Decimals

1. 1.08   **3.** .6   **5.** 8.127   **7.** .03   **9.** 25   **11.** .15
13. 554.115   **15.** 399.5   **17.** 396.875
19. 52.5615   **21. a.** 82.5 miles; **b.** 27.5 miles

2.6 Dividing Decimals

1. 31.1   **3.** 3.6   **5.** 45
7. a. 15.18 gallons; **b.** 13.82 gallons;
   c. 12.5 gallons

Chapter 2 Review

1. sum   **2.** estimate   **3.** decimal point   **4.** budget
5. dividend   **6.** product   **7.** .05; .5; 5
8. 1.09; 1.30; 1.5   **9.** .009; .05; .065
10. all the same   **11.** d   **12.** a   **13.** e   **14.** b
15. c   **16.** 4.59   **17.** 5.6   **18.** 47.6   **19.** $.75
20. 8   **21.** $3.25   **22.** 1.029   **23.** .729   **24.** 20
25. 4   **26.** .094   **27.** .98   **28.** .704   **29.** 12
30. 6.25   **31.** 60.2   **32.** .2   **33.** 35   **34.** 23
35. 590   **36.** 3.327   **37.** 2,955   **38.** .09
39. 3.25   **40.** Hiking Trail   **41.** 20 miles

42. 404.1 miles   **43.** 401.5 miles
44. No, 404.1 > 401.5   **45.** more than $15
46. more than $30   **47.** 8 miles

Chapter 3   Adding and Subtracting Fractions and Mixed Numbers

3.1 Writing Fractions

1. $\frac{1}{4}$ **3.** $\frac{2}{5}$ **5.** $\frac{2}{3}$ **7.** $\frac{4}{7}$
9. Should show 3 of 8 equal parts.

3.2 Renaming Mixed Numbers and Improper Fractions

1. $1\frac{5}{8}$ **3.** $4\frac{1}{2}$ **5.** 3   **7.** $\frac{19}{4}$ **9.** $\frac{11}{8}$ **11.** $\frac{26}{3}$

3.3 Finding Equivalent Fractions

1. $\frac{9}{24}$ **3.** $\frac{9}{12}$ **5.** $\frac{9}{9}$ **7.** $\frac{8}{20}$ **9.** $\frac{8}{8}$ **11.** 9
13. 20   **15.** 9   **17.** 100   **19.** 20   **21.** 8   **23.** no
25. no   **27.** $\frac{12}{16}$ **29.** $\frac{6}{9}$

3.4 Writing Fractions in Lowest Terms

1. 1, 2, 4   **3.** 1, 2, 4, 5, 10, 20   **5.** $\frac{2}{3}$ **7.** $\frac{7}{32}$
9. $\frac{11}{15}$ **11.** $\frac{3}{4}$ **13.** $\frac{2}{3}$ **15.** $\frac{1}{3}$ **17.** $\frac{7}{8}$ **19.** $\frac{3}{4}$
21. 15: 1, 3, 5, 15; 9: 1, 3, 9; 3
23. 6: 1, 2, 3, 6; 18: 1, 2, 3, 6, 9, 18; 6
25. 36: 1, 2, 3, 4, 6, 9, 12, 18, 36; 48: 1, 2, 3, 4, 6,
     8, 12, 16, 24, 48; 12
27. $\frac{1}{3}$ **29.** $\frac{1}{4}$ **31.** $\frac{1}{4}$

3.5 Comparing Fractions

1. $\frac{4}{5}$ **3.** $\frac{9}{27}$ **5.** same **7.** last year, $\frac{2}{3}$

3.6 Adding and Subtracting
Like Fractions

1. $\frac{3}{5}$ **3.** $\frac{1}{2}$ **5.** 1 **7.** $\frac{9}{13}$ **9.** $\frac{3}{5}$ **11.** 0 **13.** $\frac{1}{6}$
15. $\frac{1}{4}$ **17.** $\frac{9}{10}$ mi.

3.7 Adding and Subtracting
Unlike Fractions

1. $\frac{1}{2}$ **3.** $\frac{1}{2}$ **5.** $\frac{14}{15}$ **7.** $\frac{23}{40}$ **9.** $\frac{3}{20}$ **11.** $\frac{1}{12}$ **13.** $\frac{1}{6}$
15. $\frac{7}{30}$ **17.** $1\frac{1}{4}$ in.

3.8 Adding Mixed Numbers

1. $5\frac{5}{9}$ **3.** $10\frac{3}{20}$ **5.** $20\frac{1}{2}$ **7.** 20
9. a. $7\frac{3}{4}$ mi.; **b.** $6\frac{7}{8}$ mi.; **c.** $7\frac{5}{8}$ mi.; **d.** $11\frac{1}{8}$ mi.

3.9 Subtracting Mixed Numbers

1. $7\frac{1}{2}$ **3.** $3\frac{2}{3}$ **5.** $4\frac{3}{10}$ **7.** $11\frac{1}{3}$ **9.** $1\frac{1}{4}$ **11.** $5\frac{11}{12}$
13. a. $\frac{1}{2}$ min.; **b.** $1\frac{7}{12}$ min.

Chapter 3 Review

1. fraction **2.** like fractions **3.** lowest terms
4. improper fraction **5.** numerator **6.** $\frac{3}{8}$
7. $\frac{2}{3}$ **8.** $\frac{4}{8}$ **9.** $\frac{3}{3}$ or 1 **10.** $\frac{11}{4}$ **11.** $\frac{7}{2}$
12. $\frac{15}{8}$ **13.** $\frac{53}{10}$ **14.** $3\frac{1}{3}$ **15.** 3 **16.** $2\frac{1}{2}$ **17.** $1\frac{4}{5}$
18. $\frac{1}{2}$ **19.** $\frac{2}{3}$ **20.** $\frac{4}{5}$ **21.** $\frac{5}{6}$ **22.** $\frac{2}{3}$ **23.** $\frac{3}{4}$
24. $\frac{4}{5}$ **25.** $\frac{4}{5}$ **26.** $\frac{7}{9}$ **27.** $\frac{2}{5}$ **28.** $1\frac{2}{3}$ **29.** $\frac{2}{3}$
30. $1\frac{7}{20}$ **31.** $\frac{1}{18}$ **32.** $1\frac{1}{6}$ **33.** $\frac{1}{9}$ **34.** $10\frac{5}{7}$
35. $2\frac{9}{10}$ **36.** $14\frac{11}{12}$ **37.** $\frac{8}{15}$ **38.** $6\frac{2}{3}$ **39.** $1\frac{53}{60}$
40. $6\frac{1}{4}$ **41.** $2\frac{1}{6}$ **42.** $2\frac{1}{12}$ **43.** $1\frac{7}{10}$ **44.** $4\frac{5}{18}$
45. $5\frac{7}{8}$ **46.** 7 cups **47.** $6\frac{1}{3}$ cups
48. $4\frac{2}{3}$ cups; $1\frac{1}{2}$ cups; 1 cup **49.** $\frac{1}{4}$ cup
50. flour, $\frac{1}{3}$ is bigger than $\frac{1}{4}$ **51.** $\frac{3}{4}$ cup

Chapter 4 Multiplying and
Dividing Fractions and
Mixed Numbers

4.1 Multiplying Fractions

1. $\frac{1}{15}$ **3.** $\frac{1}{6}$ **5.** $\frac{4}{9}$ **7.** $\frac{2}{15}$ **9.** $\frac{1}{4}$ **11.** $\frac{2}{15}$ **13.** $\frac{1}{12}$
15. 1 **17.** $\frac{2}{15}$ **19.** $\frac{3}{4}$ **21.** $4\frac{1}{2}$ **23.** $4\frac{1}{2}$ **25.** $\frac{1}{8}$
27. $\frac{3}{8}$ **29.** 8 high school students
31. 12 people

4.2 Multiplying Mixed Numbers

1. $1\frac{3}{5}$ **3.** $7\frac{1}{9}$ **5.** $7\frac{5}{21}$ **7.** 1 **9.** $1\frac{5}{6}$ **11.** $\frac{13}{27}$
13. $22\frac{1}{2}$ doz. **15.** $5\frac{1}{2}$ doz. **17.** $3\frac{5}{6}$ feet

4.3 Dividing Fractions

1. 2 **3.** 3 **5.** 16 **7.** $\frac{1}{10}$ **9.** 1 **11.** $\frac{1}{10}$ **13.** $1\frac{1}{2}$
15. $\frac{3}{8}$ **17.** 4 rows

4.4 Dividing Mixed Numbers

1. $1\frac{7}{8}$ **3.** $1\frac{27}{49}$ **5.** $2\frac{11}{12}$ **7.** $3\frac{1}{16}$ **9.** $3\frac{3}{5}$ **11.** 3
13. 3 **15.** 5

4.5 Writing Fractions as Decimals and Decimals as Fractions

1. .5 **3.** .2 **5.** .6 **7.** .625 **9.** .333 **11.** .444
13. $\frac{1}{2}$ **15.** $\frac{2}{3}$
17. No, he only ran $2\frac{3}{10}$ miles each day.

Chapter 4 Review

1. Reciprocals **2.** simplify **3.** mixed number
4. $\frac{1}{3}$ **5.** $\frac{1}{16}$ **6.** $\frac{7}{18}$ **7.** 1 **8.** $\frac{1}{4}$ **9.** $\frac{1}{4}$ **10.** $4\frac{1}{8}$
11. 13 **12.** 8 **13.** $1\frac{1}{5}$ **14.** $\frac{2}{9}$ **15.** $3\frac{2}{3}$ **16.** $6\frac{1}{4}$
17. $\frac{7}{10}$ **18.** $11\frac{25}{32}$ **19.** $\frac{3}{4}$ **20.** $1\frac{1}{2}$ **21.** 6 **22.** $\frac{1}{5}$
23. $\frac{4}{11}$ **24.** 2 **25.** 1 **26.** $1\frac{2}{3}$ **27.** $\frac{1}{4}$ **28.** $\frac{4}{25}$
29. 35 **30.** $\frac{1}{5}$ **31.** $\frac{1}{2}$ **32.** 24 **33.** $1\frac{1}{2}$ **34.** $\frac{49}{72}$

35. 20 **36.** $2\frac{1}{2}$ **37.** $\frac{1}{12}$ **38.** 25 **39.** 6 **40.** .4
41. .75 **42.** .375 **43.** .4 **44.** .333 **45.** .667
46. .625 **47.** .5 **48.** .222 **49.** .444 **50.** .4, $\frac{1}{2}$, $\frac{2}{3}$
51. $\frac{3}{4}$, .82, $\frac{5}{6}$ **52.** .11, $\frac{1}{9}$, .12 **53.** $\frac{3}{8}$, .38, .4
54. 16 tables **55.** $7\frac{7}{8}$ ft. **56.** 18 birdhouses
57. $23\frac{5}{8}$ ft. **58.** $7\frac{7}{8}$ ft.
59. Mrs. Matthews, 2.75 hr **60.** $3\frac{1}{5}$ shifts

Chapter 5 Ratios and Proportions

5.1 Understanding and Writing Ratios

1. 86:258 **3.** 210:70 **5.** 15:4 **7.** 26:1
9. a. 2:5; **b.** 5:2 **11. a.** 1:3; **b.** 3:9
13. 60:90

5.2 Using Ratios and Proportions

1. 4 **3.** 3 **5.** 6 **7.** 20 **9.** 12 **11.** 240 minutes

5.3 Solving Problems with Proportion and Scale

1. 120 mi. **3.** 75 mi. **5.** 240 mi. **7.** 6 cm

Chapter 5 Review

1. ratio **2.** cross product **3.** scale drawing
4. equivalent **5.** proportion **6.** scale
7. 3:10 **8.** 2:1.99 **9.** 55:1 **10.** 2:3
11. a. 15:25; **b.** 10:15 **12. a.** 5:7; **b.** 7:15; **c.** 3:15
13. a. 6:4; **b.** 4:10; **c.** 72:48 **14.** yes **15.** no

16. yes **17.** no **18.** 2 **19.** 16 **20.** 10.67
21. .75 **22.** 7.5 mi. **23.** 2.5 cm **24.** 5 m
25. a. 5:24; **b.** 5:19 **26.** no **27.** $4\frac{1}{2}$ in.
28. 12 in. **29.** 270 photos **30.** 1,080 photos

Chapter 6 Percents

6.1 Writing Percents
1. 78% **3. a.** 8%; **b.** 92% **5.** .2 **7.** .03
9. .88 **11.** 1.35 **13.** 1 **15.** $\frac{13}{100}$ **17.** $\frac{39}{50}$
19. $1\frac{1}{5}$ **21.** $\frac{1}{4}$

6.2 Writing Fractions and Decimals as Percents
1. 35% **3.** 5% **5.** 50% **7.** 75% **9.** 40%
11. 80% **13.** 12.5% **15.** SportsWorld; $\frac{1}{4} = 25\%$

6.3 Finding a Percent of a Number
1. 15 **3.** 99 **5.** 17.9 **7.** 45 **9.** 8 **11.** 33.3
13. a. $1.50; **b.** $13.50
15. a. 40 people; **b.** 10 people

6.4 Writing a Part as a Percent
1. 40% **3.** 25% **5.** 20% **7.** 125% **9.** 65%
11. a. 20%; **b.** $24 **13.** 15%

6.5 Finding the Original Number When a Percent of It Is Known
1. 66.7 **3.** 48 **5.** 96 **7.** 100 **9.** 80
11. 20 goals **13.** $60 **15.** $20,000

6.6 Using Shortcuts with Percents
1. $70 **3.** 6.6 **5.** 30 **7.** $18

Chapter 6 Review
1. A *percent* is a *ratio* of a number to 100.
2. 3% **3.** 75% **4.** 22% **5.** 45%
6. 60% **7.** 5% **8.** $\frac{1}{2}$ **9.** $\frac{1}{4}$ **10.** 75% **11.** 20%
12. 40% **13.** $\frac{3}{5}$ **14.** $\frac{4}{5}$ **15.** 33.3% **16.** 12.5%
17. 13.5 **18.** 45 **19.** 20.9 **20.** 28 **21.** 25%
22. 20% **23.** 33.3% **24.** 100% **25.** 25 **26.** 60
27. 32 **28.** 320 **29.** 66.7% **30.** 23.8 **31.** 38
32. 150 **33.** 10% **34.** 9.3 **35.** 200 **36.** 33.3%
37. 150% **38.** 49.5 **39.** 80% **40.** $\frac{3}{4}$ **41.** $1.50
42. Mike and Ike CD, $14 **43.** 12.5% **44.** $12
45. $550

Chapter 7 Geometry

7.1 Identifying Polygons and Finding Their Perimeters
1. 22 cm **3.** 24 m **5.** 91 cm **7.** 18 cm
9. 280 m

7.2 Finding the Area of Parallelograms
1. 48 cm^2 **3.** 14 m^2 **5.** 50 in.^{2} **7.** 11 ft^2

7.3 Finding the Area of Triangles
1. 6 ft^2 **3.** 37.5 cm^2 **5.** 24 mm^2 **7.** 15.13 ft^2

7.4 Finding the Circumference of Circles

1. 15.7 cm **3.** 37.68 m **5.** 78.5 in.
7. 138.16 cm

7.5 Finding the Area of Circles

1. 81.67 yd^2 **3.** 28,938.24 ft^2 **5.** 3.14 cm^2
7. 4,899.19 yd^2 **9.** 145.19 cm^2 **11.** 5.39 m^2
13. 254.34 ft^2

7.6 Finding the Area of Irregular Figures

1. 203.4 ft^2 **3.** 4,875 dm^2

7.7 Finding Surface Area

1. 108 ft^2 **3.** 72 in.^{2} **5.** 188 yd^2
7. No; The surface area of the box is 1,432 in.^{2} but the area of the paper is 1,152 in.^{2}

7.8 Finding Volume

1. 252 ft^3 **3.** 803.84 cm^3 **5.** 140 in.^{3}
7. 1,017.36 yd^3

Chapter 7 Review

1. circumference **2.** square
3. three-dimensional **4.** diameter
5. volume **6.** perimeter **7.** Area
8. $A = b \times h$ **9.** $A = \frac{1}{2} \times b \times h$
10. $A = \pi \times r \times r$ or $A = \pi \times r^2$
11. $P = 42$ in.; $A = 75$ in^2
12. $P = 17$ cm; $A = 13$ cm^2

13. $P = 32$ m; $A = 64$ m^2
14. $P = 32$ ft; $A = 48$ ft^2
15. $P = 28$ m; $A = 18$ m^2
16. $P = 6$ cm; $A = 2.25$ cm^2
17. $P = 19.6$ km; $A = 12.87$ km^2
18. $P = 31.2$ yd; $A = 51$ yd^2
19. $C \approx 43.96$ m; $A \approx 153.86$ m^2
20. $C \approx 37.68$ in.; $A \approx 113.04$ in.^{2}
21. $C \approx 34.54$ cm; $A \approx 94.99$ cm^2
22. $C \approx 21.98$ ft; $A \approx 38.47$ ft^2 **23.** 53.44 ft^2
24. 32.5 cm^2 **25.** 117 in.^{2} **26.** 26.39 m^2
27. 484 in.^{2} **28.** 600 ft^2 **29.** 356 cm^2
30. 440 in.^{3} **31.** 15.63 cm^3 **32.** 301.44 m^3
33. 2 km^2 **34.** Playing Field, 2.25 km^2
35. 6 km^2 **36.** 4.71 km
37. 50.98 km^2 or about 51 km^2

Chapter 8 Statistics

8.1 Finding the Mean, Median, and Mode

1. 12.8 **3.** 86.8 **5.** 1.61 **7.** 25; no mode
9. 25; 25 **11.** 265; 265 **13.** 26 **15.** 30.8
17. 8 **19. a.** 11.43; **b.** 12; **c.** 12

8.2 Making Frequency Tables

1.

Books Read	Frequency
1	1
2	3
3	6
4	2
5	6
6	1
7	1
8	3
9	1
10	1

3. a. 7; **b.** 22; **c.** 23

5. The building cannot exceed 26.22 feet.

Building Height (ft)	Frequency
22	2
23	0
24	1
25	0
26	2
27	1
28	1
29	0
30	1
31	1

8.3 Reading and Making Bar Graphs

1. France   3. 13 medals
5. France, Australia, China, Russia, Germany, United States

8.4 Reading and Making Line Graphs

1. 550
3. Video rentals are increasing.

8.5 Reading Circle Graphs

1. 40%   3. $210,000   5. $90,000   7. A and D

8.6 Identifying Misleading Statistics

1. 14 degrees
3. Change the scale so that units of 1 degree are used.

5.

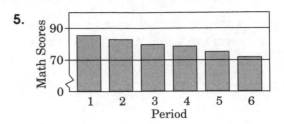

Chapter 8 Review

1. trend   2. median   3. minimum
4. line graph   5. data   6. mode
7. frequency table
8. mean: 35; median: 33; no mode
9. mean: 9.71; median: 12; mode: 12
10. mean: 1.5; median: 1; mode: 1
11. mean: .72; median: .3; mode: .1
12. mean: $\frac{1}{2}$; median: $\frac{1}{2}$; mode: $\frac{3}{4}$
13. mean: 35.7; median: 35; modes: 12 and 35
14. **a.**

Televisions	Frequency
1	2
2	3
3	11
4	4
5	2
6	2
7	1
8	0
9	2

   b. 3.85; **c.** 3
15. **a.** 900 cones; **b.** 200 cones;
   c. between July and August;
   d. Expect September to be lower than August.
16. **a.** 17%; **b.** $3; **c.** $4.20; **d.** Distribution and Selling
17. 457.5 cars   18. 436 cars
19. 400 cars, Sweden
20. 560 cars, United States

Chapter 9 Probability

9.1 Finding Outcomes of Games

1. heads, tails **3.** 1, 2, 3, 4, 5, 6, 7, 8
5. 1, Red, 2, Yellow, 3, Blue, 4, Green
7. The game is fair. There are 18 ways to get an even sum and 18 ways to get an odd sum.

9.2 Finding the Probability of Events

1. **a.** $\frac{1}{6}$; **b.** $\frac{3}{6}$ or $\frac{1}{2}$; **c.** $\frac{1}{6}$; **d.** $\frac{2}{6}$ or $\frac{1}{3}$; **e.** $\frac{3}{6}$ or $\frac{1}{2}$;
f. $\frac{6}{6}$ or 1
3. $\frac{5}{100}$ or $\frac{1}{20}$

9.3 Making Tree Diagrams

1. kind of juice **3.** 6
5. **a.**

Hamburger — Juice, Milk

Hot dog — Juice, Milk

Taco — Juice, Milk

b. hamburger, juice; hamburger, milk; hot dog, juice; hot dog, milk; taco, juice; taco, milk

9.4 Multiplying to Find the Number of Possible Outcomes

1. 6 outcomes **3.** 288 combinations

9.5 Finding the Probability of Independent Events

1. $\frac{1}{12}$ **3.** $\frac{1}{8}$ **5.** 0 **7.** $\frac{1}{6}$

Chapter 9 Review

1. Probability **2.** outcome
3. sample space **4.** Independent events
5. fair game
6. **a.** $\frac{1}{6}$; **b.** $\frac{2}{6}$ or $\frac{1}{3}$; **c.** $\frac{3}{6}$ or $\frac{1}{2}$; **d.** $\frac{3}{6}$ or $\frac{1}{2}$;
e. $\frac{6}{6}$ or 1; **f.** 0
7. **a.** $\frac{2}{8}$ or $\frac{1}{4}$; **b.** $\frac{1}{8}$; **c.** $\frac{5}{8}$; **d.** $\frac{2}{8}$ or $\frac{1}{4}$; **e.** $\frac{3}{8}$
f. $\frac{2}{8}$ or $\frac{1}{4}$
8. **a.** large cup, small cup; large cone, small cone; **b.** a menu in an ice cream store
9.

H — H — H: H, H, H; T: H, H, T
    — T — H: H, T, H; T: H, T, T
T — H — H: T, H, H; T: T, H, T
    — T — H: T, T, H; T: T, T, T

10.

R — H: R, H; T: R, T
B — H: B, H; T: B, T
G — H: G, H; T: G, T
W — H: W, H; T: W, T

11. 30 outcomes **12.** 24 outcomes **13.** 8 ways
14. $\frac{2}{10}$ or $\frac{1}{5}$ **15.** $\frac{3}{20}$ **16.** $\frac{2}{8}$ or $\frac{1}{4}$ **17.** $\frac{2}{20}$ or $\frac{1}{10}$
18. 0

Chapter 10 Integers

10.1 Writing and Comparing Integers

1. ⁻4 **3.** ⁻15 **5.** 5 **7.** 7
9. 3 is greater than ⁻3 **11.** 0 is greater than ⁻5
13. 4 is the same as ⁺4 **15.** ⁺6

10.2 Adding Integers

1. negative 3. positive 5. ‾16 7. 2 9. 0
11. 10 13. ‾22 15. 0 17. 20 19. ‾15
21. ‾20 23. ‾2 25. ‾7 27. ‾15 29. ‾24
31. ⁺1

10.3 Subtracting Integers

1. ‾19 3. 24 5. ‾2 7. 50 9. 30 11. ‾10
13. 18 (or 17) floors

10.4 Multiplying Integers

1. positive 3. negative 5. ‾21 7. 24
9. ‾48 11. ‾25 13. ‾45 15. 256 17. 24
19. a. ‾8°; b. 6°

10.5 Dividing Integers

1. positive 3. negative 5. (‾64) ÷ (‾8) = 8
7. ‾5 9. ‾13 11. 1 13. ‾5 15. ‾3 17. ‾1
19. ‾6 lbs.

Chapter 10 Review

1. positive numbers 2. opposites 3. integers
4. absolute value 5. negative 6. ‾45
7. ⁺2,356 8. ⁺25 9. ‾150 10. ‾62
11. ⁺12 12. ‾35 13. 42 14. 75 15. ‾30
16. 0 is greater than ‾7
17. ‾10 is greater than ‾2
18. 3 is greater than ‾12
19. ‾5 is greater than ‾9
20. 12 21. 7 22. 4 23. 33 24. ‾26 25. 12
26. 0 27. ‾7 28. 60 29. ‾8 30. 75 31. ‾100
32. ‾18 33. ‾20 34. 0 35. ‾5 36. 4 37. 17
38. 30 39. 0 40. ‾14 41. 10 42. ‾1 43. ‾48
44. 12 45. ‾10 46. ‾2 47. ‾24 48. ‾28
49. 30 50. 4 51. ‾6 52. 90 53. 0 54. ‾60
55. 80 56. ‾27 57. ‾140 58. ‾5
59. 3 60. 3 61. ‾45 62. 4 63. ‾1 64. 5
65. ‾4 66. 4 67. ‾24 68. 10 69. ‾6
70. ‾5 71. ‾15 72. 48 73. ‾6
74. Wednesday 75. 25° 76. 9° 77. ‾3°
78. ‾1° 79. ‾12°